THE MARTIN BORMANN
DOG CARE BOOK

THE MARTIN BORMANN DOG CARE BOOK

poems by

Michael R. Brown

Resolute Bear Press
Robbinston, Maine

No part of this publication may be reproduced or transmitted without the previous written permission of the publisher, except in the case of brief quotations in critical reviews and reviews.

Cover design by Valerie Lawson, Vallon Design
Cover photograph by freddie marriage, London, UK

Resolute Bear Press PO Box 14
Robbinston, ME 04671
207.454.8026
valerie.lawson@maine.edu
resolutebearpress.com
facebook.com/resolute.bear.press/

ISBN 978-0-9988195-2-5
second printing

Printed by McNaughton & Gunn, 960 Woodland, Saline, MI

Contents

Citizenship 9
    The Acorn 10
    Archeologists 11
    Alexander Maxwell Garrison 12
    Frayed Plaid Robes 13
    Matins 14
    Comparatives 15
    The Blue Door 16
    Before the Great Depression 17
    Tea 19
    The Colorado 20
    Weather Watch 21
    Any Summer Day 23
    The Aluminum Helmet 24
    One Voyage 26
    Another Metropolis 28
    The Fisherman 29
    Empty 31
    Winners 32
    Repairs 33

Color 35
    Deterrence 36
    The Shortest Month 38
    East St. Louis, 1917 39
    The Fiery Furnace 40
    Collaboration 41
    Envy 42
    Crossing the Street 44
    The Brown Bug 45
    Can You Sing? 46
    Runagate 48

Miss Brooks... 49
Native Art... 51
28 THINGS FOR WHITE PEOPLE TO DO
DURING BLACK HISTORY MONTH...... 52

Money 55

Brookline Ladies 56
The Potter's Mistress 57
The Hot Shot Café 58
Room 59
Fins 60
Three Loons 62
Kaddish 63
Hard Times 64
Rusman's Gallery 65
Star Dance 66
The Lady Who Coils the Cables 67
Happy Day 68

Politics 69

Spring 70
The General Direction... 72
Komarovsky 74
Mournful Wail 75
La Lecture a la Robbe-Grillet 77
Forget Paris 78
No Defense Needed 80
Killers 81
The Comedian 82
Gloria Lynne 83
Catherine the Great 84
The Badger and the Bear 85
Mary Magdalen 86
Tender Analysis 88
The Emotions of Dreams 89

Cro-Magnon ... 90
Don L. Lee at the CCCC ... 91
Pop! ... 92
Parents Held Hostage by Hatless Teen ... 94
Word Problems ... 95
City of Night ... 96
Chusok ... 97
Man and Souperman ... 98
Human Engineering ... 99
A Pleasant Young Man ... 100
Galileo's Apology ... 102
Frederick Douglass ... 103
Delta Evening ... 104
The Martin Bormann Dog Care Book ... 105
Over and Over ... 111
Face It ... 113

War ... 115

King Philip's Head ... 116
In Memory ... 118
The Whiskey Rebellion ... 119
Gettysburg ... 120
Dry Tank ... 122
All Quiet ... 123
Turtles ... 124
Dave's Cave ... 126
The Last Nightmare ... 128
What Old Men Know ... 129
Absalom, Absalom ... 130
At the Table ... 132
Priests' Skulls ... 134
Like Kings ... 135

ACKNOWLEDGEMENTS ... 137

BIOGRAPHY ... 141

Citizenship

Was he free? Was he happy? The question is absurd: Had anything been wrong, we should certainly have heard.
   "The Unknown Citizen"
      —W.H. Auden

The Acorn

for Ron Lettieri, one year after

It's a small thing brought down
by a storm, solid and bright green, presaging the oak it could
        be
with the right mix of water, sun,
and enough dirt to keep its lofty growth
from becoming too proud,
the sort that hosts small creatures,
exhales tons of oxygen to sustain
the rest of us on our daily rounds.

It reminds me of a friend who wanted
a stone as a gift from my travels
and got one from the old city of Jerusalem.
Another asks, "Why do we do these things?"
Because they are nobody's job.
Like the Chinese poet, like water,
we settle in lowest places
where none would care to go, s
ustaining all by giving ourselves away.

We can build dreams and philosophies
from small things fallen to the ground,
the old stone, the young acorn, a puddle,
a friend in mid-life—milestones
showing how far one came,
how far all of us must go.

Archeologists

Studying the dead is a romantic occupation.
Archeologists invest the virgin sacrifice with noble motivation,
honor slavery with civilization.

Most of us don't want to do it all over again,
get enmeshed in that giddy, uncomfortable dynamo
opening ecstatic depths where emotions boil over
and cloud heady possibilities with smoky reminders,
sulphurous hate.

If we go through all that,
it must be with someone new,
diving into other passionate depths
even if they lead to the same ends.
We'll settle for ashes from our own fires.

Our reveries are not imaged in bone.
We don't find forests in leaf prints.
We ignore mounds of dust that tell us nothing is forever.
We have spent eons growing upright and facing forward.
For all our brainpower, we resist historical fact,
let our emotions make us myopic,
remember two-ness as a golden age.

Like a child by the seashore,
I give all my attention to digging on this beach,
my back to the waves,
great cities a sea journey away,
as if these piles of sand will amount to something.

Alexander Maxwell Garrison

York, Maine, 1660

Aye, prisons and garrisons,
When the door shuts,
You're in or you're out
And no going between.

I built this one for
A civil war. You may say
That's *nae* this, but
Who *canna* choose to fight?

I would *ne'er* want *ma* children
Otherwheres when others come;
That's in each board and beam
Chimney brick and hard shell coat.

Round heads or feathers make
Na difference. When we're gone
And one goes after another's land,
This garrison will stand.

Frayed Plaid Robes

While my father strutted ghostlike
on the broad ramparts of his life,
his greatest truths lurked in dark corners.
The more he thought he knew what was around,
the more realities scurried along the edges,
quick furtive things he could only guess at.

In his last days my father saw farmers move
in weird dances where only corn shocks stood.
He dodged imaginary slaps
and cars that never came down the street.
He talked to people across the room
as if they came from different worlds.

I walk into the VA hospital every Monday
and stare my future in the face.
Ashy old men shuffle past in frayed plaid robes,
cigarets burning down to yellowed knuckles.
They mumble meaningless conversations
with absent passersby in vacant hallways.
Someday I'm going to be a shambling phantom
in an unfurnished future.

I fear the loss of fire, but the nurses tell me
that, drugged and alcoholed, these men
never felt the rage to dare life's tightropes.
Still, I get an attitude about the broad
daylight truths that scare us into doing right
while the tough rat-like facts of life
gnaw at the foundations, pick at
the threads on the frayed plaid robes
until we stand naked and alone
in front of our graves wondering,
How did we come to this?

Matins

Watery faces in wavy mirrors
match gravelly voices turning rough words
till the look behind the reflection clears
and we see ordinary signs of everyday people—
pimples, nose hair, lines and small rosy
bumps waiting for age to drain our vigor.

The face over there responds to water's pure
feeling, urges us to human actions until
we put on clothes, get practical, arrange our
lives, do right things and become fools.

The fresh light of day illuminates our
best side; we can imagine almost any
possibility except what will happen
before noon, how we will slouch at five,
in what dark place we will fold
wrinkled visions of night's invention
and lay it away with failed intentions.

In this seam between waking and day's drag
we see how we slip between the rock
and the hard place, how tomorrow's
waking will be someplace else,
where we will stand above another basin
and in a new mirror meet an older face.
Small imaginings such as these
show us the damage we do to ourselves
with every rough encounter of ordinary days.

Comparatives

We talk to our computer screens
just the way cavemen talked to their fires.
Twilight presages tomorrow's storm.
Many things that happen we do for ourselves.
We pin hopes on the moon's pull,
beg it for inspiration, regret those footsteps,
the tire treads that follow, small scars to no purpose.

Some consequences seem inevitable while
we pretend they will never occur. Others we accept
as if direct efforts—
sunlight's glow on your bright hair, as though
shampoo had nothing to do with it,
the hit of pheromones so immediate
we forget learned associations and think
the thing itself must be deep in our brains.

We fall before we lose our footing.
Strange dogs bark in our darkest dreams.
Children hide in the rubble of homes.
Real nights are never opaque as we imagine,
while real days may never be clearer than we can see.

The Blue Door

Low cloister doorways bend pride.
A rabbit hole where plaster oozed
between laths like frosting,
or the inside of a rough-hewn doll house
or the backs of theater flats.
Planks rest on beams
above cloudy insulation.
One window in the end wall
shed light to see by but not examine
portraits less distinct than frames.

One day I walked in,
shut the door,
and heard the latch snap.
My grandmother's Victorian temper
taught me that this was not a room to stay in.
So I turned and kicked it open.

Down in the basement
and down on my knees or up in the attic
into what others have set aside,
because those who put them there
are only ready for us to see
when it doesn't matter if we do.

Slick magazines hidden out of place,
a serious book with a mysterious cover,
its contents so much
knowledge no one wants,
but the stuff everyone has
and needs to know everyone else has, too.

Before the Great Depression

I

Hugo clomped to the table, shirtless,
suspenders down about his knees,
pants drooping, undershirt already damp.
The bulb from the ceiling's center glared
off his smooth white head, set his brows ablaze,
added blackness to the shadows in the caves.
Lena scuffed from the stove in slippers, set
the egg plate, poured coffee
in the china mug, the back of her house
coat a curtain rung on conversation.

His hands hung like castings.
He sat like stone. She sighed, the effort
to keep upright focused on her lower
back, her pelvis, supporting arch atop
the pillars. He took the heaviness out
to work, and night was ended.

II

She woke to the slick touch of soapy water,
thought of bathing in it, but when
the dishes were done, Jack came with the milk
and came in. By eight she was giggling
at her silly feet jiggling above
his back, the arch stretched counter to its stress,
and paused to touch for, oh, just a second
the wet patch in the center of the sheet.

Hugo beat his weight into the metal,
each awkward elbow trimmed in the smashing
press, made right by frustration.
By lunch the bright spots where the pips had been
were suns. All afternoon he stood, swayed,
a husk in hot wind, his eyes unfocused,
the bang of the press a distant thresher.

III

She stopped in the middle of cutting cabbage,
wiped her hands, and lifted her breasts
to see if she could make them feel the way
they had when she laid them on the butcher's
as he set the meat on the counter.

Hugo went for whisky to clarify
the foundry dust and buy a week
for his working years. He nodded to
Kate, made excuses, went up
the outside stairs. As fast as he
got his pants off she was lying in bed
with her legs widespread, unready for him.

IV

He pushed and drove, and when he had an inch, reared,
fires deep in the caves, and thrust, dragging
dust and pubic hair into her. He forced
and pushed with only once a slight
withdraw for further purchase, and went home.

Lena smelled the beer from Friendly Eddie's
and met his flush with a blush of her own.
When he patted her rump, they looked
forward to a quiet night alone.

Tea

This dark cup of serenity,
the color of good English ale,
is but a pre-scientific way
to kill microbes. Such small
wonders establish civilizations.

Bodies have settled,
see possibilities, rub bones
into artifacts, daub buffalo
on walls, leave handprints—
great leaps from the addition
of one footfall to a stone floor.

Distance from cook fire
to table lengthens, but shortens
Picasso's reach for the wine.

The Colorado

> *"If you have the same problem in your third marriage, you have to start thinking it's not them."*
> —Chris Chandler

The broad river meanders in wide valleys,
plains before it came.
My clogged head seeks
poetry and tea to cut fog and mud.
Summer's hot rising air
draws moisture from the Gulf.

No matter how focused the lens,
how certain the facts,
once history's truth is told,
we all become fiction—bad guys, victims,
the righteous brother, the supreme—
as surely as a river bed once set speaks
among low eyeless hills of intimacy past.

Weather Watch

> *"If the ozone hole holds this summer, do you think we can go back to Lake Superior and see the Northern Lights reflected in our faces again?"*
> —Ed Morales, REGT

    Chickadees chirp in the pines;
    doves hoo in the prairie grass.

My back to Crow Agency, facing the Custer Battlefield,
the brown rolling grasslands falling away
to the badlands, a golden falling star shoots an arc
in the purple sky, and I wonder whose auguries to
read. Whose medicine man can tell tomorrow's outcome?
Will the warriors astride their ponies merely watch
Long Hair pass up a chance to feed his vanity?
We depend on the basic truths:
those who look for trouble find it;
the peaceable ones will someday fight.

    Catbird sits on the chimney top;
    bobwhite hides in the sage.

The sailboat man on the lee of the great lake
cuts sausage rings to fall next
to cheese on waxed paper. Garlic pinches
my nostrils. What will the weather be?
A sailor who can't read wind shifts,
low clouds scudding over Thunder Bay.

    Terns pinwheel in the cove;
    gulls float on the lagoon.

Mist dissipates among stony mountains
by the East Sea; ox carts directed by patient
farmers' hands creak up muddy roads,
heads capped by peaked toweling; broad pants
swish below brocade vests, and the morning
calm softens the beer-drinkers' laughs

at lunch, leaning against a paddy wall, watching
changes that whisper a new season
will insinuate itself in twenty days.

> Cuckoo mournful in the lindens;
> magpie laughs by the road.

The porch looking out on the Java Sea
frames tropic light in bamboo edges;
the ocean tugs and shifts gently;
rain falls at night. Even with radio codes,
satellites, and all-weather channels, any good boat
can get pounded in open seas and driven away from home
 where a fat wife waits too well-attended.

> Kestrels spin on the storm front;
> cormorants splash in the bay.

Our nature severed from Nature,
we try with electronic extensions
to perceive what is open to us, stumbling
into dark canyons, crossing broad ground
to see where nothing interrupts our view,
the most ephemeral weather slapping our eyes,
and miss all that would answer each
everyday question.

> Sandpipers dance on the ocean's edge;
> waves become pelican slides.

Any Summer Day

Clouds scudded in bunches,
gray bellies threaten to burst
but mostly dripping and hurrying on.
The sun came back like a hot hand flat on our heads,
stirring hay and honeysuckle up our noses,
opening our ears to cicadas and swallows.

A twenty-minute whoosh rampant
in sea-blue streams carried Popsicle rafts downtown,
washed the air as clear as Bockenheimer's window,
and arced a rainbow from the river where we couldn't go
to a place too far away from town for us to
get to on our bikes before it disappeared.

Like other pre-adolescent mammals, we dug up dirt,
chased ourselves in open fields, climbed, swam,
and at least once, tried to fly.

August afternoons, with school threatening
like purple evenings making baseballs hard to see,
skinny boys with close-clipped hair climbed
bridge supports, crawled into gardens, teased dogs,
and ran the periphery of girls the way we skirted civilization,
moving from one side of town to the other through the woods.

Twice a week we reveled in brilliant tourmaline
swimming pool waters, screaming in joy,
springboarding cannonballs
aimed at any girl without wet hair,
hopping to pop music across hot concrete
for ice cream sandwiches and raspberry snow cones,
the big clock in the pavilion
no more use than a soft drink sign.

A few died, but out of sight,
mysteries we postponed till lonely winter nights
made us look for unsatisfying answers in books,
afraid to ask anyone who would tell us the truth.

The Aluminum Helmet

Above the glasses tinted to screen out UVs,
it was probably a Kangol cap covered by aluminum foil.
I startled him out of his trance with a warm hello.
He backed off because he knows that Earth people
who understand him want to put him away,
and he doesn't know when aliens will show up in human form.

Transmitting radio messages through his fillings,
extraterrestrial beings are telling him to do bad things,
like "Kill the President. Only he prevents your people
from joining the family of the universe."

This one man chosen to do the work of superior beings refuses.
A shell-shocked gentle man stock still by a duck-infested pond
defends our civilization by holding to a basic value.
We must not kill individuals for any noble collective good.
And he fights the aliens by himself
because their voices never leave him alone.

Somehow he discovered that an aluminum hat muffles the
    orders,
but just now he was arrested by a static burst
reflected off the water's surface and up under the helmet.
Freed by my friendly gesture, he will walk quickly to his room
and bang his head against the wall until the voices stop.

But he can't hold out forever, and we had better help him.
Because the voices don't only tell him to kill presidents.
Over in the medical center a doctor experiments on babies.
A teacher abuses children. Poets poison people's minds.
Yet all the urgings of the fascists in the galaxy
can't make this lonely man kill one of us.

He won't let us mummify him in a charity mental ward.
He holds out as long as he can in fear that when he is gone
a weaker soul will become their pawn.

And on a late-night drive across a high bridge
one of us will see him tight-roping the rail,
throwing the devil's last temptation back in his face:
"If you are the great power of the universe,
lift me up so that I may do your service."
And the aluminum helmet will spiral away in the wind.
He will fall, and the world will have
just one more night of unmurdered sleep.

One Voyage

in memory of Jason Miller

His hammock up in the fo'c'sle
hung under wet wood holding
bugs and dirt and a terrible smell.
Least skilled, most expendable,
he did the roughest work,
climbed highest in worst storms,
and spent off time topside,
watching the dolphins run.

By a natural gift he improved the work.
Tested by the elements, labor,
and a cat's cradle of social connections,
he returned from his first trip with a full share.

A second voyage would have pitted
him against himself, knowing that
everyone works in foul weather. To decide:
captain early and always at sea,
or get to business in a rocky port,
with fat wife, noisy kids, bills to pay.

What can we say to a beautiful lad
who worked with ease, beat the odds,
and bought an annuity of warm drink
in a cold city? For 25 years
his craggy face, stunned expression,
and cloudy gaze were locked where
a crafty man docked a ship in a bottle
and rowed a dory in a glass.

> *Have a care then, handsome men*
> *who sail out early on easy ways.*
> *For all the golden beads of light,*
> *no treasure, no more to recite.*
> *He sits where lamps are only steady;*
> *and the time of his days is always night.*

His face pales as wood ages.
A youth disrupts his stupor and earns
a torrent of abuse in an incoherent gale.
So the news of his death comes late,
well past the seven years the song
gives the shipwrecked. His empty seat
fills, as seagulls harry the wake
picking the catches he could have had.

What's the sadness in that? Except
our long eyes knew his nimble feet and mind,
black hair tousled above clear eyes,
and a smile to charm the devil from the deep.

> *Have a care, lovely men,*
> *to whom the ways come easy.*
> *For all the golden beads of light,*
> *no treasure, nothing to recite.*
> *He lies where lamps are always steady,*
> *the time of his days forever night.*

Another Metropolis

Once again I've put myself in an anonymous
room in a foreign city, alone, without language,
skill, smarts or sense—just my dogged persistence.
I spend the quiet night huddled
around my gastro-intestinal tract, hoping
to cure my distress before morning.

By 10 AM I'm plowing through crowds on the Bund,
waving away postcard sellers and money changers,
hanging over the parapet to watch sampans in strings,
undeterred by the foul smell of garbage thick on the fetid
Haungpo. By early afternoon I'm on the side streets
off Nanjing Road, flapping one sandaled foot in front of the
    other,
dodging wash hung out on bamboo poles, weaving among
street sweepers with shorthandled brooms, delighted by the
aroma of steaming lunches scraped from tiny bowls.

On nervous energy, outcries of "foreigner"
no more to me than the buzz of cicadas in the poplars.
I'm stirred by the smiling child, a 19th century tower,
chimes! Just before dinner, my new friend
August Sheng points out the flag of the International above
the Russian embassy, tells me about the jazz band
at the Peace Hotel, and how the taxis go.

Twelve and a half million people raise a lot of dust.
The air never clears, the summer sun never sets,
night sneaks in while I sip tea in my room,
and darkness falls when I am already deep in sleep
flat on my back. Up at dawn to watch
the city wake, behold its arteries lined with trees, see
the boulevards clogged by bicycle riders in faded shorts,
old t-shirts and conical straw hats,
to get shanghaied just by the wonder of it all.

The Fisherman

I drag seines through fishy scenes
and catch a perch or two,
casting each net as wide as I can,
then with steady pull of seasoned hands,
muscled back and salty arms,
dragging them in.

I love the great lucent dome,
fecund dirt, and many waters.
Creatures attract me,
whether they flick quick tongues in dry air,
leap across dusty grass,
wind through barely visible currents in dark water,
or lie back on cheap beds,
arms above their heads,
long legs akimbo,
enjoying the stretch that ends with shakes
like a wet dog settling into relaxation
that leads to slack muscles
and slightly engorged nether regions.
When I think of the loss of such things,
my sadness becomes unbearable.

I take up the net of words,
barely wider than my mind's breadth;
I heft, hold, and swing it spread full
to fall on pieces of the world—
silvery fish leaping in bright air,
a coyote trotting along a Yellowstone road,
long fingers with clear nails drawn through
auburn hair aglow by a bedside lamp—
each treasure a world in itself;
all these worlds within a world.

I try to pay my way,
create art that shows us what we have,
but I get more than I give,
fear my voracious life will outlive

the deaths of all I want,
and I will die,
a fisherman drowned in words,
without fish or sea or sky.

Empty

The closed restaurant with dishes and decor,
flatware,
the wooden seahorse by the door,
empty because no one is there.

At harbor's end broad golden sand,
shorebirds,
gulls and the constant work of the wave's hand,
speak to a town bare without words.

A hotel without guests, a classroom
on holiday,
each knows it will have its season soon,
even the mortuary on a happy day.

But now nothing occupies us like
the dead;
nothing promises what will strike
or cures the sadness of an empty bed.

Winners

Churches depend on our need to give,
winners count on adulation, else only those
driven to subjugate others would compete.
Where can we find the one who wants
to win for others, the church of the non-dependent,
the victor who distributes the spoils?

I'm not talking about a high culture identification
with Diego Rivera, Isaac Bashevis Singer, Wole Soyinka,
Rabindinath Tagore, or Yasunari Kawabata,
not rooting a hundred years too late for the redskin
team at an easy win or noble disaster on some grassy field.

I mean the transportation that brought you here,
this microphone, the ways of an American bar,
what to wear on a summer day,
how to eat, quench your thirst, look
or not look at those around you.

They are not in this town,
the priests who pass the plate
filled with cash for those who need,
runners who honor the crowd that cheered them on,
trophy winners who set to work
to make the next victor's monument.

Repairs

Corn stalks bound to his shins,
the small child in the new straw suit
climbs to the volcanic table top.
His black eyes shine with pleasure,
his knotted hair bobs and sways,
and he dislodges an obsidian face from the mesa.

Rivers of air stir the land,
corrosive dust shields the planet,
and molten rivers overflow valleys with fire.

The child in the straw suit stomps,
scattering ashes of the last cataclysm.
In the long night, Hurricane and Maya
dance till their bitter healing spirits rend the sky.

Color

The only reason I am black is because you are white.
—*James Baldwin*

Deterrence

Left to their own devices, lovers
meld confidences to resentments,
bent over satin vanities, molding alloyed
projectiles, or sit cross-legged
on chenille spreads rubbing scraps
of trust into sharp pellets,
wisps of smoke making red-eyed squints
by which they sight the lethal ends
into beloved aliens, like vampire hunters
yearning for torn flesh, splintered
bone, pierced hearts, or they bide
their time in backwaters of oppressive
regimes, scheming till banks open,
heat cools, the chief's jeep rolls
into the *Zócalo*.

Big-eyed Bonnie Parker fills casings with
the gunpowder of love turned back on itself.
Ma Barker with twisted mouth fits shotgun
shells into cold tubes with caustic thunks.
The schoolmarm spins the chambers of a snubnose.
The singer forces another round into the clip.
In a moldering, frustrating jungle of desire,
a full-lipped *rubia* centers her passion on the
insertion of copper-sheathed fifty calibers
into canvas loops.

One low pressure, half-moonlit night
when *el jefe* thinks it's all right because
la Señorita has calmed, while his eyes linger
on the fire for an absentminded moment,
she slips the special out of her purse,
aims the automatic at the back of his skull,
angles the shotgun below the belt,
sets the machine gun on rapid fire,
flashes on organs exploded
by bloody hydraulic force,
listens dream-like until the rattling stops,

the hammer clicks one final time on oily steel,
then wonders what the fuss was about.
Just another man gone.

The Shortest Month

12% of the people
shout at 80% who
become deaf for 28 days
because somebody has decided that TV,
public forums, and retrograde bookstores
will push stock they wouldn't touch
unless a riot was coming down the street.

Crescent red cells catch in capillaries,
dam arteries of African Americans,
swell limbs, clog organs, cause stroke,
and no one can stop it;
nobody knows when it will kill.

Racism is white folks' anemia,
debilitating spirit, deforming soul,
killing those who do not carry it.

East St. Louis, 1917

For generations we tended white folks and a white crop.
When they got machines, they turned us out.
Rain ran off hard ground; I never expected flood and drought.
So we moved near the cities till they made us stop.
Our men worked in the mills and women did the same
Things we always did—cleaning, cooking, child care.
We went to church and were happy with our share,
Until work slowed, and new white folks came.
They half ran through town—mean, noisy, liquored up;
Used guns, chains, and clubs to kill the men.
When they came through again, fire followed them.
Once more they kicked the women and beat them up.
But what kind of men with what evil desire
Will throw a crying baby back into a fire?

The Fiery Furnace

    Shadrach, Meshach, Abednego,
not a test, but an expression of it.
    Kings, Herods, Pharaohs, and Caesars
built elaborate tortures, but persecutors never know
    the martyr's peace of mind, and sometimes,
God protected his children in miraculous ways.
    We are rid of most earthly kings
and powerful men persecute children still.
    Hang, cut, burn or beat, and He
performs an occasional miracle—
    the voice bubbling out of Emmet Till
after his tormentors thought him dead,
    his chained body rising on the waters,
his sorrowful mother putting his body on display.
    What white people call for surcease
from wrongs their darker brothers cause them?
    They tempt beauty with wealth, buy talented
souls and waste their lives, except God lifts prophetic
    examples who rise clean and fly.
Miscreants in vicious groups still loop tree limbs,
    plant stakes, build ovens, and burn believers.
Amid fiery furnaces stand pure gentle ones
    who do not burn because they know
the sanctuary of His hands, restraint of power
    calling forth majesty that rebukes
the meanest by its presence alone. Already tested
    beyond human endurance, churchgoers stand
in the ashes, the holiness of angels composed
    in the easy terrible expressions of faith.

Collaboration

      Geological remnant of old centeredness,
              the magnetic pole
    guides the expedition to its pinnacle, draws compass
    quivering on its post, a sliver in a bowl.

Peary and Henson cooperate in twilight,
            could not survive
with any but the other this height,
mating eye and gravity till photographers arrive.

In the *Tribune* they look like Hilary and Tenzing,
            the dark one framed
by the arm of the shadow achiever, sensing
above him the peak that neither named.

A glossy from *The Defender* commands the grand-
            children's forced gloom;
his sons know only the shadow master stand-
ing on the pole, a casket in the living room.

No daughters run to peaks, but fly
          alone a while
and fall on foreign islands from the sky;
while he was grim, they must forever smile.

      All beginnings are auspicious we say,
            lying at dawn;
    like lines of magnetism through the arc of day,
    I point inside your circles and press on.

Envy

for Gregorio Gomez

I envy the Chicano poet, not that skinny
Chicago Renaissance man with slick hair, dark eyes,
and thin grin, that neatly dressed *clarinete*
with smooth talk and hushed music, not that one.

And not that old *pachuco* from LA, *la guitarra gorda*
with the cross tattooed above the junction of his thumb
and forefinger who learned to cut men's guts
and swell women's bellies before he was fifteen
and now lives the quiet domestic life of love and poetry
with a wife so beautiful as the be the envy
of all Chihuahua. Not that one.

I don't envy that big Chicano with the two poems
he only wrote in his life, the guy who pours tequila
like piss and drinks it like a sacrament, the one who
sings the blues and married white women,
that big trombone of a man with too much trauma
and a bone as long as the Baja. I don't envy him.

But I do envy that brassy little trumpet in baggy pants and vest,
el hombre de la poesia, with long curly brown hair
who shuffles around and poses like he owns the fucking world.
I envy that little bastard whose every philosophical
statement begins and ends with "What the fuck, man."
That one who's got a lame excuse for everything we do wrong
and who never turned a wrong phrase in his life. "He's great.
Go ask my friend." The one who is so sensitive that the hint
of ragging him in poetry brings out great bellows of protest
and who will probably deafen small children for blocks around
when he hears this—*sin no está borracho*. "Ask my friend."

He intones his trip through the city in some low-riding *cucaracha*,
and knows all the bros. He's got a dozen names.

He believes time is still told on stone tablets,
believes the sun belongs to Mexico,
eats nobody's shit, and lays out a banquet of his own.

I figure, if I'm really good in this life, if I drink a lot
and at least talk about screwing everything that moves,
in the next life I can come back like that—descendant
of corn growers, pyramid builders, curbside car mechanics—
a sawed off, insensitive Chicano who can call a meeting,
never show up, and not give a fuck.

Crossing the Street

You or I step into the crosswalk,
eye the driver, demand the right of way.
But some dare not challenge traffic,
lest drivers force them to the curb,
cut close, and spit or scream.

I hear words I haven't heard in years.
A guy in the Stop & Shop says loudly to his wife,
"He was a typical nigger." I tell him to watch his mouth.
He sees no one with me and wonders what's my problem.

For years I had an odd shield against this profanity.
Now I hear the private talk, the casual everyday
aimed at nobody, but woven into conversations
as readily as random curses, fear,
pop culture condemnations, or cold contempt.
I'm caught in the middle of the street
by threatening vehicles no one else can see.

The Brown Bug

I crushed the brown bug in a blood rage
and his insides smeared in an uneven line
lumpy and colorless across the page,
but his back remained unbroken;
the deep broad color edged away
as chestnut does to that point
just short of where the perfect tone lay,
that magic strength of dark brown and black
perfectly blended on an unbroken back.
        If I had a back like that
        I could carry the world—
        and call it black.

Can You Sing?

When I was 20,
the tenors did "Little Girl Blue"
over "Good King Wenceslaus,"
the way she sang truth over melody.

When I was 30,
a woman 10 years younger and 20 wiser
sneaked me into her ex-boyfriend's chocolate room
where we made love all night to two albums.
I never thought it was okay
to do it accompanied by the concert for Dr. King,
but as a response to death, sex always feels right.

When I was 40,
I wore out a bootleg of "One More Sunday in Savannah,"
scratched, badly recorded, more truth than music.

In my 50's
a budding literary star
stopped a Supreme Court Justice and his wife
who walked in late. "Nina Simone,"
the man behind me whispered.

Her CD's played when she died in Paris.
I can't imagine how free France must have felt,
but I hear the wisdom
when white folks explain and sympathize.

"I Want a Little Sugar in My Bowl"
was first performed before she was born,
yet her defiant version
is the one played on legendary jukeboxes.
What did it take to sing feelings true

when the piano gave the lie to her voice,
when recordings hurt her ears as much as praise,
so out of time with their ways?

I hear that on the box,
and the voice in the back of my head
says, "Nina Simone."

Runagate

Azaleas burn; fruit blossoms explode;
dogwoods bloom in East Tennessee; cows rest
next to sleepy black calves on green carpets;
forsythia reach high beneath so light a load.
Clouds hug hilltops and bright sky sheds light rain.
Low fireworks, each vibrant bush and tree gets
its singular show, and damp wind wets
river's gray winter coat, spotted and plain.

Follow the flowers escaping slaves were told.
Surrounded by verdure, without drinking
gourd or north star, was it enough to know
that distance, running, no shout and no snow
were the signs of freedom itself, thinking
already the sequence of spring so bold?

Miss Brooks

> *"I would ask nothing better than to see more clearly,*
> *but it seems to me that no one sees more clearly."*
> —Merleau-Ponty, *Primacy of Perception*

She dresses like a school teacher,
and her spindly legs
lean at angles to the podium;
her chin points above the audience
and her voice follows her eyes,
rising and ebbing over the people
in longitudinal waves;
she wears her hair like a cap.

She touches her thumb to her tongue
and speaks through old photographs,
aged monochromes in sepia
of Chicago before he grew tall
and of his mousy women
whose brass was dull
when they walked slow.

The newer pictures contrast sharply.
The boy has grown
and his women walk staccato
(even old ladies learn
to walk staccato, too).
She fingers the gloss lovingly, yet,
unable to forget the quiet past when,
just before war was declared
on the bus driver,
she could be angry
at being herself.

Did you notice
how her shoulder blades
seemed to have slipped
halfway down her back?
But her jutting jaw

tucks into her shoulder
and her bulging eyeballs
push at the slits
and demand respect.

Her fiery photos
may still be found
sheening the walls
of paper houses in panic,
and in the embers,
on two angular charcoal sticks,
a nearly burnt-out schizophrenic.

Native Art

Just before the big art show
        they murdered the last sculptor
        in the Yukon Territory.
If the Mohawk build a skyscraper on their land
        the first sixteen floors
        will be under water.
No Cheyenne ever wanted to wear Custer's
        buckskin suit:
        it's bad enough being red and blue
        without looking white, too.

                Why can't I put my wanted posters
                in the post office?

Madam, those shoes have not been worn
        since they were broken in
        by the Sioux boy at the Pine Ridge factory.
The Pawnee are trading ponies for beards
        so they can establish profitable communes
        on National Forest lands.
The Turquoise Kid vacationing in Taos:
        today's version of Custer's expedition
        for gold in the Black Hills.

For Sale: Picturesque Condominium Apartments
        Apply: San Isleta Pueblo

Four cases of snake bite per tourist season
        seems a fair admission charge
        to the Crow Indian Heritage Center.
At the original Esalen Institute
        everyone who went fishing
        caught enough to satisfy his psyche.
If the Seneca offer is still open, I'll send my sons:
        Harvard has yet to meet the demand
        to make men of them.

A little big man can beat a crazy general any day.

28 THINGS FOR WHITE PEOPLE TO DO DURING BLACK HISTORY MONTH

1. Take a white friend to lunch and talk about our problem.
2. Read a poem by a black writer who is not Langston Hughes.
3. See a movie by a black director who is not Spike Lee.
4. Create a local chapter of Racists Anonymous:
   "Hi, I'm Mike, and I've been a racist all my life."
5. Keep a Black Muslim publication for bathroom reading.
6. Sit with black folks and listen.
7. Learn about the red, black and green.
8. Remember why the Underground Railroad had to be underground in the North.
9. Reverse at least one cliché a day. Get whiteballed and black washed. Experience the whitest day of your life. Tell a little black lie.
   And maybe you can sing the whites.
10. Don't expect one black person to know everything about every other black person.
11. Look at black people like you know them even if you don't.
12. Stop worrying over Freddie Gray and think about what you have in common with the cop who drove the wagon.
13. Listen to an entire speech by Minister Louis Farrakhan before you express an opinion about him.
14. Trace the migratory path out of Africa that caused our ancestors to turn white in adaptation to a colder climate.

(*Valentine's Day*. We could stop here. If white people did half of what we should, we could solve the whole problem. But we know how likely that is.)

15. Join the campaign to put the face of Frederick Douglass on Mt. Rushmore.
16. Learn the first verse of "Lift Every Voice and Sing."
17. Stop calling black entertainers and athletes by their first names.
18. Name one black scientist.
19. Name two black astronauts.

20. Say three black prayers.
21. Don't ever try to speak Black Urban English.
22. Never again say she looks like a Black Audrey Hepburn.
23. Keep your hands off folks except by explicit invitation.
24. Don't think being a basketball fan or listening to rap
    cures you of the disease of racism.
25. Stop trying to cover your awkward embarrassment with
    cute expressions. Even we don't believe
    we're truly sorry
26. Don't pretend to know how any great black leader felt.
27. Read *Beloved*. It says the problem with white people is
    that they never know when to stop.
28. Plan to do these things for 12 months.

And for Leap Year, stop calling this
    the Land of the Free and the Home of the Brave.

Money

*If you work for wages,
you belong to the working class.*
—*U. Utah Phillips*

Brookline Ladies

Brown-haired with mouths buttoned down,
doing conventionally useless things that connect,
like the crew beading at the front table,
the knitter inviting every poet and singer to dive
into her large brown eyes and swim his or her way out.

They gesture with thoughtless certainty,
knowing beyond conviction what they command is right.
They were made for the resurgence of folk music,
cede unbowed allegiance to lyrics aimed beyond
their cotton clothed presence while melodies lift
them in mindless concentration on hand tasks.
Children of blood suckers, lieutenant generals of motors,
grandchildren of coupon clippers with railroad names,
their ancestors ragtimed while orphans froze in the snow
or suffocated in mines and spinning mills;
now they sugar baby food and hook Third World kids
      on formula.

A stringent phrase catches them like a bad smell
or rich food stuck in their teeth,
but in their perfumed lives they tough it out,
and the nuisance passes as easily as they buy
tickets to Oxfam fashion shows, flick away TV images
of skeletal Africans with flies on their eyes, or drive Volvos
past old men sleeping next to shopping carts under city bridges.

The Potter's Mistress

It's the clay that forms the potter's hand,
    patching cracks, building grooves across fingers first,
    turning on the wheel hands into hands till
    one night he hears the hollow clink
    of his arm against the workroom sink.
That's the way the potter's owned
    (we see the cleft on sculpted stone and miss
    the bluntness left on hammering fists):
    clay malingers underneath the fleshy maul,
    forming slowly in return, the illusion
    of success in form drawn out of earth,
    hardening the potter most of all.
It's the same for red-eyed astronomers,
    machinery men who make our cars;
    thrown on the wheel, cultures inferred from shards,
    the artifacts say these men have been made our way;
    they are the amphorae raised when one no longer
    knows the music of the Plain of Jars.
That's the net effect of setting matter in motion:
    the scraped hollow up to the old man's skinny neck,
    the rasping echo of his damp insides,
    the glaze on ochre skin, fit finally
    for decorative effect and stiffened play
    (brown breasts those bowls under the
    peasant blouse of the potter's mistress there,
    and beneath her skirt. . .well-urned, you'd say?):
The potter only thinks he molds the clay.

The Hot Shot Café

Asheville, North Carolina

On the last counter stool Dee
studies her sore leg,
muscles inflexible stone.
She will need this work
for as long as Mom has done it.

When she walks, her knee turns out,
pain shoots to her hip. More than Mom,
more than the bright-eyed daughter
stopping the word "ass" and saying
"butt" for the old ladies' benefit,
Dee has deep sadness in her eyes.

Her mind failing, Mom runs faster.
Dee has always hoped for a house,
a man to help her body tone.
The few who stuck long enough
to cause real trouble left
this sad, growing resistance.

Mom pitches downhill. The young
one bounces high on rubber soles.
Dee cannot find any path but
the one she has already walked
stretched ahead as far as she can see.

Room

She looked at home
in the brown light
of the dust-painted room.
As soon as I opened the door,
sucking the raw wind
under the window frames,
the sleepiness
and the metallic coffee
bothered me the more.
Her fingers buttoned
the cross-hatched overcoat
which padded the grainy desk top
for her fuzzy head.

This was my classroom;
how could she
get there so early?
make me the intruder?

She didn't move,
and I went in quietly,
shuffling my papers,
hoping she'd wake
before others arrived.

"Why do you come here so early?"

"I wake myself up
as soon as I can,
and the first thing I do
is get out of the house.
You don't mind, do you?"

How could I tell her
I hated her for it?

Fins

It's a Fifties year,
what nobody who lived it
ever got nostalgic for.
A distant dad sat president
atop a military-industrial complex,
built pipelines and highways,
accepted Supreme Court decisions,
and threatened the world with radiation.

We took cotton, coffee, cheap labor, oil,
and anything to make metal.
We gave rock and roll,
chewing gum, and blue jeans.

In the middle of that gray time,
like sunflowers on town dumps,
there sprang fins—
bright, gaudy, metallic, useless,
ineluctable fins!

First they were nubbins
holding short stacks of tail lights.
By '58 they were front fenders swept
back in huge pointy panels,
steel sheets sculpted and shiny
as the chrome on a Colt revolver.

Such exuberance in the night—
dashing streetlight reflections
like the spinning globes
on Klatu's whirling peace ship,
and just as futile!

Heavy metal names were Windsor,
Monarch, Studebaker, DeSoto—
an American assortment of Detroit iron
powered by gas-burning mills
on new concrete expressways.

What bright joy in a futureless time!
That flashy excess disappeared
with one lift of a young man's hand.
Dad departed, and the next night
we marched into was lighted by
burning stores, searchlights, and napalm.

Now it's Brittany, Nike, and Gap—
same old shit, only capitalized.
The sheriff's tin star is backed up
by a holster full of smart bombs.
The businessmen who own the government
use it to steal crude and ore,
stack the cash on islands they own.
The night is lighted by external combustion—
gas flares, phosphorous, burning oil—
and none of it reflects anything but itself.

When that flashy Fifties roar carried us
to the hollow promise of the next small town,
we were dazzled by baked enamel pastels,
but now we know what's driving us,
and we can't go fast or far enough
to get away from that.

Three Loons

Forsythia bloom, poplars bud,
but the old oak tests spring's intention.

In a kennel at Fairhaven,
three oil-soaked loons lie on a tarp.
Subdued like abused children,
they don't cry or shift or twitch.

More birds gather in clear water.
Swans sail farther upstream.

Why should we clean the loons
when soon the tarp may be loaded
with roseate terns, trussed and basted,
like squabs ready for broiling?

Triage postponed because we crave electricity
and can't lift our eyes from computer screens.

Kaddish

Young poets fuss about who will
get the Nike commercial, MTV spot,
how media moguls will enslave their
fresh rants and newly-formed longings.

Pave the way out of Compton with
eight million dollars and watch
a rapper lose his revolutionary edge.
When he gets shot, he's already dead.

The greatest poets of my generation
succumbed to institutes and universities,
ensconced themselves in personalities
on the *cul de sacs* of pop culture:

Greenwich Village and New Orleans in the 50's,
Provincetown and San Francisco in the 60's,
Key West and Missoula in the 70's,
played out, laid back by-ways.

A burnt-out schizophrenic has
not been cured but institutionalized
so long she is harmless: Diane Wakoski.

The long list of those who haven't written
anything good in 25 years begins with
Mary Oliver, Billy Collins, Seamus Heaney,
Hans Magnus Enzensbarger, and Robert Pinsky.

Hard Times

I have visited a country that once
had all its trees stolen. A nearby nation
marched in and took them to build homes.
The conquered people built their lives
out of dirt, water, sunlight and air.
"Trees die on their feet," they said.
They remembered how palms bend
to absorb the storm's fury. Their thoughts
ran deep as oak roots spreading
in the tough earth as widely as its leaves
permeate the easy sky. They practiced
humility like the bonsai which
lives hundreds of years by not growing.

When those once-conquered people were free
and had food and shelter, they planted trees
on every clump that could hold a seedling.
Today you can see a nation of glorious cities,
tight farms, modest highways, and richly
wooded hills where all the trees grow in rows.
In the hearts of the forests stand temples,
and people walk to them as we do to cathedrals.

Recently I sailed to another country
on a trading ship built from tall trees
carefully selected to last one hundred years.
The leaders of the once-conquered nation,
who call themselves children of the ashes,
have sent their industrial legions into
the shipbuilders' jungles to mow down trees
for office furniture, fake antiques,
and chopsticks. They cannot hear what the trees
taught their parents: tyranny won't last;
the world is not so easily replaced;
when we are successful, we must heed the lessons
of hard times. Trees teach us what we can be.
Our enemies show us what we will become.

Rusman's Gallery

It's a sure sign to stop shopping
when I think I've been here before,
but that one cheap batik wouldn't rest
till I put it in my bag. Like some
fin de siecle Parisian art dealer,
I try fifty places in the sunny country
seeking impressionist light to brighten city rooms,
unaware of Van Gogh at Auvers,
but convinced that he must exist.
I no longer notice colorful birds
perched on pink rings inside purple ovals.
Every Ramayana in ocher has the same lack of effect.
When I see only crimson, yellow and
brown in one room, I sit down.
It's all the same, but it's his.
One lane away, the herniated
old man in *The New York Times* waits.
It hurts to haggle with an artist,
but he handles it well,
bent among cartoon cattle staring wall-eyed at the sun.

Then in dim rooms a young woman
with a patchy-haired child astride her hip
endures bargaining to gain baby food.

I stroll through the bamboo fence
and into a room filled with brilliant panels.
A luminous banner three meters long
holds a Javanese dream character carnival.
It knocks me back on the bamboo bench
next to Rusman who says,
"It's the only one in the world."
My eyes are greedy but my wallet is poor.
I gape, pray that hope will spawn some means,
and tear myself away.
Now nothing looks any good.
This is how art defeats money.

Star Dance

In a wicker chair at the Panorama *losmen*
looking out on Pangandaran Bay
where the night is always twelve hours long
and the Southern Cross dances as awkwardly as Orion,
 I'm angry that science has digitalized the sky,
compensated for waves in the atmosphere,
pinpointed stars and the magnitude of starshine.

In South Java where days are not electrified and nights
have no recorded music or the blue glow of television,
I feel like Wordsworth in the Lake Country,
know why Van Gogh went to Auvers,
putting streetlight grids and sooty cities behind
and getting drunk under the starshot canopy.
Fresh air picks up the scent of a cracked palm branch,
coconuts split on the beach.
Noises are quarter notes on the sea breeze bass clef,
Javanese indistinguishable from waves and trees.

For all its invisibility, I don't want
to believe air fakes the star dance.
Once that fact flowers in Eden
I feel the broken wicker poke my seat
and know what Romantics run from.
I smell decay in the jungle,
hear coughs in the huts,
start to think.

A googleplex of galaxies away
on a planet just like this
fish nets dredge up plastic bags and bottles,
beach kids cut their feet on pop tops,
the forest floor has turned to red dust,
all water is sewage,
and there's no point in getting home before dark.

The Lady Who Coils the Cables

Like one of the three Graces who decide our fates,
the lady who coils the cables from the drag seines
sits on the beach, two piles up as far as
her conical straw hat, a basket behind her.

Her flowered blouse flaps in the breeze.
Striped sarung wrapped tightly around her knees,
she watches my neighbors with contempt.

Cultures clash and we find ourselves at loggerheads:
they refused the beggar and fed the dog.

Happy Day

The pitcher on my porch says,
"Love in heart, Dream in living."
The radio in my head plays, "Oh,
Happy Day," and I ask how much
more do I want than this?

brilliant sunshine   oh, happy day
pale green ocean   happy day
jungle foliage boats on the shore
beautiful Javanese stroll by my door

Once I ask, tho, I want you
here with me. The Javanese
want more fish, less sickness,
a better start for their children.
Dream in living, Hope in heart.

We industrialized ones need these
simple reminders, like the art
of the fruit seller offering bananas
when I have some and she has none.
Dream in heart, Love in living.
Oh, Happy Day!

Politics

If voting could change things, it would be illegal.

Spring

A dry spring wind carries yellow dust
from the Gobi Desert to South Korea,
and blossoming student actions push
riot police away from campuses,
memorializing the Kwangju Massacre.
      My American students flock to Fun Flicks,
      pretend to be Chippendales,
      and believe the Vietnam War was a Nixon trick.

"Deng Xiao-ping is dead," students murmur
in mournful derision in Beijing streets,
haunted by childhood visions when a great
cultural flowering was cut down
and fields as far as the eye could see
showed only chopped stalks.
      My students cast ballots for which DJ
      to hire for Spring Fling, believe JFK
      was king of Camelot just after Richard Lionheart.

      Distance makes it all so safe.
      We purchase freedom with credit cards of lost memory,
      ski mindlessly on mountains of ignorance,
      treat history like a lost dog.

Yesterday SLORC laid martial law on Mandalay,
the people at their mercy because rice stockpiles
bought weapons for goons to use on Buddhist priests.
A slender flower, Aung Sun Suu Kyi stands alone
in a barren rice field, her face tilted to fading sun.
      I help my students find 31 great figures
      to fill the calendar for Women's History Month.

Poets, when was the last time
you wrote a word to break a chain?
cast a verse in a tyrant's eye?
asked a simple question to set a twisted principle straight?

held out a poetic line to some hopeless one?
helped foolish children learn the truth?
> Spring is the time to dedicate yourself to renewal.
> If you begin this night, you won't regret tomorrow.

The General Direction...
    if you catch my drift

for Craig Nelson, The Cantab, July 11, 2001

Shakespeare turns into Euripides;
I hate not giving him the time he needs,
    The great bard who fused
        Language and action,
          Comedy and history,
    The profound and the lewd.

    Like some rapper,
Richard Burbage shifts his codpiece,
    Trying to be dapper,
His body an instrument,
    In this case a lute,
Plucking his own strings,
    All sound and salute.

"So, Will, how shall they fancy this new one?"
Will replied, "If fame were but a day and gone,
We might as well wipe ourselves
On the pages and toss them away,
But what if 400 years ensue
And a student says,
    'I love reading him;
    I hate having to;
    And at least that Burbage knew
    How to sport a codpiece.'"

"I get your point," Burbage said.
"I find yours too hard," was Will's surmise,
    Like a modern poet,
    Loving to hoist himself
    On his own petard
    And trying to get laid
    By quoting the Bard.

Students, forsake repetitive classrooms,
      Monolingual translators,
      Dullness professorized,
      And introduction praters.
Let performance be your codpiece;
      The more fulsome
The less likely they will see us as we are:
      Big rants,
      Little talents,
      Shameless lust
      Empty pants,

Lines already written
      In what you haven't read
May yet help you find your way
      Into some else's bed.

"Not an entirely bad proposition," Burbage said.
"But Kyd and Marlowe were men of knowledge,
both of them went up to college."

"We're more famous than they will ever be,"
Will replied, "and we're all long dead.
But thank God our fate
Is not in today's hands or verbiage."
"Or codpieces," said Burbage.

So, English majors, take heed of texts and classes,
As long as you can tell the horses from the asses.
      Poets with reps are worth the reading.
      Poets with raps are worth the heeding.
      Slam poets are worth their pleading.
      But don't miss my point:
      It's always something else these poets are needing.

Komarovsky

La Chiquita of 31 Flavors shook her knee-length hair
back of her shoulders and opened a wide smile.
"You look like a teacher."
She wore a shirt big enough to cover my car
and jeans painted on her pipestem legs.
Her big brown eyes brightened,
and she scooped extra Jamoca Almond Fudge on my cone:
"Where should I go to college?"

One of my ex-wives said I was like Komarovsky,
the decadent old professor who seduced
Dr. Zhivago's Lara at Moscow U.
Maybe you remember some guy
who was probably 35 when you were 20
and always had coed nymphs
prancing round his maypole. That's not me.

I've known women profs with double-wide couches
who screwed every hardbody in their classes.
But when the greatest rosebud gatherer
in the history of Illinois—Chicago took my class,
she read the newspaper. The sawed-off son-of-bitch
who led the attack on my tenure
fucked one woman into Oxford and another into suicide,
but I couldn't close my office door
if Margaret Thatcher were inside.

It's the guys who love their students who don't,
while the cold-blooded bastards fuck them every time,
a lesson many women also seem to learn.

Mournful Wail

Yesterday it was Marnie.
    "Why do they hate me because I'm a Jew?"
A year ago it was Angela.
    "Was it because I'm black?"
Three years ago Kathy wrote,
    "Are all men so cold?"
Five years ago it was Lee Seung Jae.
    "Gook. Slope. Why this hate?"
Every year I read the same essays.
    "I have lived my childhood among these white men,
      and suddenly they reject me, hate me, call me names."
I taught those white people Shakespeare.
    "Hath not a Jew eyes? Hath not a Jew hands,
      organs, dimensions, senses, affections, passions?"
I've taught them Pygmalion.
    "I sold flowers. I didn't sell myself. Now you've made
      a lady of me I'm not fit to sell anything else."
I teach them Steinbeck, Ellison, Baraka and Morrison.
I get back "The Female Eunuch" and "The Fire Next Time."

On July 4th, 1856, in Rochester, New York,
Frederick Douglass said, "I hear the mournful wail of millions."
After that war removed slavery's shackles,
    smug Northerners cackled at poor whites and over-
    looked
    the consequences of their righteous abolition—
    as long as one of us is enslaved.
Today I hear a mournful wail in our cities.
    While the elite complain we use only 1/10 of our brain,
    they lead a society whose most fertile imaginations
    have been paved over with their worst intentions.
And for the many thousands gone I find only one
    November cotton flower, one rose in Spanish Harlem,
    one tough sunflower stretching up through barren
    concrete slabs to clutch at pale urban sunlight.

30 years ago it was Ben.
    "What difference should my religion make to them?"
25 years ago Cheryl said, "Why do they look at me that way?"
I hear the mournful wail of millions,
    and it is not their fault
    that it will not stop.

La Lecture a la Robbe-Grillet

    She's the sort of woman who feels that repeating what she has just said reinforces its importance when there was no importance in the first place. The audience knows perhaps in general what she knows, but there are certainly a few who do not, and she will tell all of us. When she repeats what she says, we will all feel that we are getting more out of what she is saying because the repetition will make us consider at a deeper level even though there wasn't any importance in the first place.

    The accompanying audio-visual presentation allows her to read to the audience what she has just said for those who may not have grasped the fullness of it under the pretense of setting straight what she was saying so we do not miss or misconstrue what she was telling us its importance which bears repeating although there wasn't any importance in the first place.

    Thus we have a conference slot filled by someone who dresses in a conventional way that is supposed to suggest importance and to em- phasize the importance of repeating the conventional in a way that, while thoroughly conventional, she repeats with that repetition will cause us to look more deeply into the subject and grasp its fundamental importance when there was no importance in the first place.

    Many layers of data—a veritable truckload of loose straw—encase the melon of conventional verbiage holding the seed of an ordinary idea as a way of reaffirming the importance of something that wasn't important.

    The speaker feels she is losing her audience because her point is so difficult, so she breaks down the obvious statements into parts and re- peats the parts as parts, occasionally gathering the parts already repeated by repeating them as larger chunks, creating more levels of supposed im- portance

Forget Paris

Somewhere in long journeys we go native,
take on the ways of those we are among
or become what they believe us to be.
We return to whom we were,
our senses altered by a foreign perspective,
strangers in every land, most of all at home.

We declare this to be our final shore,
yet doubt we will stay here always.
Once tethered in a foreign place,
we are never quite so bound by origin.
Knowing the drift of islands in the sky,
we find summer cloud dreams not so free.

When the universe clicks like a great clockwork,
we may say, do, or dare all with impunity.
No matter how twisted my maxims,
you will find truth in them if you believe
that everything works to some good end.
It's only when the world has lost purpose
that we fear to look madness in the eye.

If all can be lost, anything can come to naught.
When all is sound, anything will do.
In Newton's universe we are credited
with horse sense by being truly absurd,
pursuing the logic to its greatest extremes.
His great thought was not the apple's fall,
but the force extended beyond the tree.

If the precise Chinese checkers of our fate
may be tossed in a box and rattled by a brat,
we rightly live in fear of our least word.
Woe to those who win the game and anger the child.
Relax, young Gullivers; act up, old men.
the world is neither the great golden clockwork

you suppose nor the capricious nursery you fear.
Its boundaries, like all good fences,
keep logic from straying beyond sense.

In Paris you saw neither the world's skin up close
nor the chimera of constellations scattered in the dark,
but merely this rude beautiful place
with sufficient order to keep us safe
and enough mayhem to call us to play.
Rest a while;
wake willing to take another chance.
Return our smiles without so much thought,
and join us in the dance.

No Defense Needed

A snotty prof at Lake Forest
says Pound is not popular
because he was a fascist.

I say,
T. S. Eliot's Anglican religion
hurt his poetry a lot more,
and he wouldn't have been
nearly so great without Pound's editing.

Whittier wrote a lot of bad poems
about the abolition of slavery,
and the college they named after him
graduated Richard Nixon.

Neruda wrote more powerful poetry
because he was a Stalinist,
and the people who criticize political poets
never listen to them.

These English professors are always
looking for a way to cut somebody down.
It's their fascism we ought to worry about.

Killers

A chambermaid in the Hotel Carlos told me
Richard Speck was the quietest, nicest resident in the place.

When a Wilson Avenue drunk reels into the Siam Café,
blinking uncertainly as if we are the surprise,
the patrons chase him.
Blood from a deep gash in broad rivulets around his split nose,
he sways in shoes stuck to the floor
until a customer growls, "Get out."
The drunk tries to focus.
"Get out," the diner barks,
and the derelict swings about with shabby grace
and sails into the cold night.
But in the poetry bar we can't distinguish
machine gunners, cyanide lacers, and gay clown killers
from those parts of ourselves
that we set forth.

Listeners respond to the worst disasters
like traffic reporters on talk radio:
"IDOT tow trucks are having a tough time with that load of
    steel
on top of the burning school bus on the Kennedy this morning.
Better figure an extra half hour or pick an alternate."

A madman bursts through the tavern door—
Thorazine rumbling in his blood,
wild-eyed with stubble all over his head and chin,
a broad diagonal scar across his face,
looking like an escapee from Dr. Mengele's experiments,
he drools raw words and kicks an invisible dog.

Our eyes fixed on the taciturn reciter
baring deep soul secrets on the stage,
we should watch what we're doing,
exposing the dark sides of ourselves
while the real killers walk anonymously among us.

The Comedian

    for Haki Madhubuti   (Don L. Lee)

I look for that hungry, fiery-eyed
skinny kid in a long coat peddling
poetry pamphlets under the el at Sixty-
Third Street. He's somewhere in
the quiet voice, the baleful stare,
hands without anything to do, feet flat,
never a twitch. This beanpole in baggy
pants looking offhand and saying hilarious
things that nobody hears refers to
the stock market crash as White Monday.

Telling people things too hard for them to hear,
being Mr. Absolute Lee, maybe they don't
listen. Maybe every tough voice
speaks in the wilderness, and things are so
bad he doesn't have to shout to be heard.

Gloria Lynne

Honey, I can do it all.
I played Atlantic City with a 40-piece orchestra.
I told them we're going to take it right down front.
I worked with the four boys real close.

They love me in Philly.
All my records come out there and they sell big.
They sell in Europe, too,
but most of all in Philly.

When I'm talking about the 60s
I mean when I was doing "Am I Blue" and "My Funny Valentine."
You understand? My 60s.
I can fit my voice into that like a soft hand in a suede glove
and move the music from inside.

That one-note thing that I do that puts you to sleep?
That's not the trick, honey.
The trick is what happens before that.
It's just like soothing the baby.
It's all in Bach's "Goldberg Variations."

I didn't get here being some little black girl popular in Philly.
When I take the stage,
it's what came before that wakes you up.
I know all the music of the 60s,
the 1760s, too.

Catherine the Great

Being a princess is a pleasure;
being a queen means work. Her father
spoiled her. She idolized him for it,
and none of us can measure up. She only
wants what she can't have. If she can
get her hands on it, it's spoiled.

Forever twelve, she's perpetually
waiting for presents to be delivered,
her wishes to become commands,
her pleasures nobody's business.
She makes love like one molested as a child,
all push and pull away, hold tight
and withdraw, the ecstasy bringing on
painful memories so deeply rooted that
each time she conquers them anew.

She has to have a room of her own,
a servant, a rich father with a lot to do
elsewhere, and nobody is ever allowed
too close. Her dreams predict
a world which must be given to her
because she has no control over it.
That is daddy's business. He
must bring her what she wants.

"I want what I want when I want it"
must be the motto of princesses
from time immemorial. Boys and girls
forever read the same fairy tale
differently. Prince Charming
wants Cinderella because she has not
been spoiled. Cinderella believes she
has earned the right to be
an imperious queen. It's the
missing piece in Lear—
why he spurned all his daughters.
Even when we are close to them,
they act like somebody else's children.

The Badger and the Bear

"He does a lot of good things, but he's not a good man."

With dour rectitude, he is right.
One look at my amorphous exterior
and you know I don't give a shit about
form, fashion, front or restraint.

Guys like us have been in every revolution in the 20th century:
Villa and Juarez, Mao and Chou, Johnny and Mitra.
He can't trust himself;
I can't suspect everybody.

"The horse has the bit," he cries.
"All, all will be lost!"
I hang on, my ass bouncing high,
and laugh at the crazy ride.

For people like him they invented tables, chairs,
government committees and porcelain toilets.
I can't be the perfumed dowager.
I'm Queen Min, the joyous fucker
who knows what's in people's hearts is all right
because if it isn't, it will kill them.

No flags for me!
I'm a man of blankets, animals,
and whatever they drink in the fields.

I have to get my hands on things,
stick my tongue in and taste life's deepest flowering recesses.
Red meat to last all night long—
or I'll chew you up, too.

Mary Magdalen

I became a whore for religious reasons.
I take up collections and minister t
o my needs. Who else but a whore
would believe a man rising from the dead?
The bread of this body has sustained
so many and not diminished. These net
stockings catch men as neatly as any
Dead Sea snare. And better than
The Book tells us, I know who
to keep and who to throw away.

Take that man with the scar angled across
his cheek to a ragged wiggle under his chin.
Like women who get burned and survive,
no matter how smooth they are elsewhere, you
can't touch that bad unyielding place.
Some of us are like that inside.
Hurt once so bad, we don't go looking
for trouble, yet we're durable at one
point in a totally unforgiving way.
While soldiers dominate the strong,
nail them to boards in torturous deaths,
shoot dice for the robe and move on,
we bloodwise meek ones inherit the earth.

I know all the streets of this empire,
all the bedrooms, all the tricks
we play with our bodies to shield
us from ourselves, thinking that when
we go under in emotion or let others
come into us in devotion, it's a good
deed to allay the evil we do every day.

I have no names that last, no hopes
beyond a modest home by the sea
and an old age when I won't have to
sell my death to be free. Any afterlife
would be a bonus of pain. If it's only

spiritual, I'll miss the best part
of my pleasure—that I had something
men needed. How many can say that?
If we go to some Paradise where we
romp in everlasting joy, I've had my
share. Blessed are those who hunger
and thirst for justice sake, for they
get fucked like all of us—just when
we had some hope. Anything I can
do for a man takes three minutes.
Everything else is talk.

Tender Analysis

He punched the base of his throat.
"Cherry cough drops," he said.
"I don't know why, but
they get me right here."

"So you know all those things
we did were okay," she said,
an arbitrary limit to high demand
of shower imagery she recalled
three years ago, these too often
places of pain she can't endure again.

"I can't remember anything
before I was eight. Show me
pea soup and I throw up."
So the adult has only preferences—
soft clothes, dull colors, fast talk,
hours in the gym with the gloves on.

"I didn't remember till all this
stuff came out in the newspaper,"
says the self-destructive lost child
who molesters left behind,
careless about smoking and drinking,
wary of easy touch and church authority.

The Emotions of Dreams

"In my dreams there are superfluous people."
—Jeff Paris

The great scary Easter Island faces of our childhoods
diminish as we grow. Baleful stare becomes the right cast
for father, mother's cool charm charming no one.
We invent systems of dream interpretation,
build Pantheons, label boxes in the garage.
Haunted houses, where demon aunts laugh at severed heads
 and uncles reaching with fat piercing fingers become
Disneylands with mechanical arms waving out of crashed
planes, and we smile at how silly they are.
Innocuous nuisances get magnified. Dustballs become bugs,
mites garish metal growlers with hard teeth and sharp feet.

Television is our philosopher's stone.
History, tragedy, character and invention
are transmuted into bite-sized cereals
with the same tint, tone, and pace to every construction,
working the rough-edged material of life into
flat, flickering, muffled narratives every child can comprehend.
We note the skill and criticize the game.
When there is war, we believe we saw it.
When there is peace, we click on a sitcom.
The teenage retort makes our friends a laugh track.
Useless people doing nothing in the upstairs apartment
have become our standard, and nobody scares us anymore.

We neglect those who sit and watch,
forget that families have no extra people.
Just as the newly-found neutrino has no mass,
no attraction, yet builds everything,
the unperceived asserts our ignorance.
It is not that they do not matter—are not matter—
but we who are not sharp enough to know it.

Cro-Magnon

I have built the bookshelves and sit on
the deck slathered with sun tan lotion.
Below, my partner rattles dishes and I get that
contented feeling that comes with home cooking.
Sunlight fills the house
except for one dark room.

We live with a Neanderthal,
a loping, low-browed, dark-eyed
bone clubber from the Olduvai Gorge.
All day long he hunkers morosely in his cave
chanting weird syllables to complex rhythms
he beats on the floor with blunt tools.

He speaks no language that we know.

He makes short daytime forays
into our larder, and at night he scours
the city in his hunch-backed stride,
jaw hung low, dark eyes sweeping alleys,
hunting and gathering, feeding until late,
coming home in silence, growing larger.

Soon on an early morning bathroom walk
I will stumble over a large foot in the hall,
his cave grown small, back and knees
forcing out the walls while he sleeps.
Our fridge will become a tin can,
our pantry a snack. When he learns
our language, his first word will be *meat*.

I believe that parents' fears created civilization.
We must feed, tame, and educate
our children before we starve,
and they become cannibals.

Don L. Lee at the CCCC

Wet-lipped and bending,
pelvic bones and nipples
tugging their bodies toward the podium,
women await the ascetic
young poet's presentation.

At his first words they slide,
press down on their chairs
and push their arms ahead
with a slight enfolding.

Men appear profound,
lower lips push forward
and hands emphasize high foreheads.

He reads his well-written rap
and stands his ground
in the cultural space
defined by the rostrum
and 300/30 years.

Faces fall
to annoyed passivity.
Women's lips curl
as though they have sucked sour grape;
they squirm like they have
sat too long in wet underwear.

Pop!

Quick! What do the following five people have in common?
    Genghis Khan, Aristotle, Gilda Radner, Harry Houdini,
    and Angie Dickinson?
    They were all subjects on *Biography* last week.
The theory of information glut states that the more we get and
    the more it connects, the faster we lose it.
    Anything more than three years old is ancient history.
Roll the tape.
Like an IQ test or SAT,
    Jeopardy values quick recall of specific information.
    The logical result—a nation of lawyers!
Pop goes the culture.
Our weakest link, George W. Bush descended from an oil line
    to win Ben Stein's money.
    Whose line is it anyway?
In the 60's Chuck Braverman made film montages
    that covered the previous century in 60 seconds.
    Who were all those people on *Laugh-In*?
Now that Hip Hop is history,
    smoking a mystery,
    and our lives longer,
    our computers have a half-life of 4 Mhz.
The expert in colonial woodland warfare
    has ceded his telephone to his teenage daughters,
    but he can't contact his Revolutionary War re-enactors
    when his Compaq is down.
Soon we will credit Julia Child
    (who said of pies, "Nobody likes a soggy bottom.")
    with being mother of the Soggy Bottom Boys.
Elizabeth Taylor *was* Cleopatra
    so she and Caesar were contemporaries,
    and Michael Jackson burned while Nero fiddled.
    Who's afraid of Virginia Woolf?
I'll take "Kings" for $800, Alex.
And the answer is "Late Night Television."
    Who is Johnny Carson?
    Who was Jack Paar?

   Who was Ernie Kovacs?
    Sorry, that was Jerry Lester.
When we have no past (Oliver North),
   we have no memory (Ronald Reagan),
     and pop culture washes away our sins (Josef Stalin),
    we depend on the quick-answer people to answer for us.
    Just live long enough Slobodan Milosevic.
Television taught my students that Viet Nam was a Nixon dirty
    trick and when the American people found out,
    they impeached him.
It was never our line, anyway.
If you've got something to say,
   you don't get your 15 minutes of fame.
A great spiritual leader of an ancient religion,
   Frank Zappa, son of Winston Smith, said:
   "I look out my window, and I know that's real.
   I look at my television, and I know that's not real.
   And I never confuse the two."
Punch the cultural reference and listen to the laugh track pop!

Parents Held Hostage by Hatless Teen

He filled the doorway without threat
yet determined to hold his line of want.
With bruised eyes and underslung jaw
he didn't stand a chance against our unity.
No childish charm softened our heads
as long as his cheeks were discolored,
his puffed lips slow over dogged rhetoric.

Knowing we had been fooled
when we discovered the second deception,
knowing our son had put a price
on his head with the hat he'd bought
as soon as he hit town. We drew the line:
no team hats, no starter jackets, no gang colors.

Now, desperate to look like everybody else,
his body filled our doorway,
but we had him right where we wanted him,
stretched out in front of us
instead of lying at the feet of Latin Kings.

Word Problems

My grandfather's favorite:
>if it takes three bricks to sink a gumboot in a barrel of
>pudding, how many tin cans will it take to cover the
>poor house roof?

If you can salvage 90,000 bricks from a blasted mosque in
>Mostar, how many vacant windows can you brick up,
>leaving just one gun port for a 14-year-old sniper
>to shoot women on their way to market?

If half a million well-armed soldiers cannot subdue a peasant
>population of seven million, how many militia
>will it take to silence women in America?

If two cops in Providence can get away with killing a cop
>they know, how many can kill one they don't?

If six Boston cops can beat a fellow officer in plainclothes so
>badly that he is hospitalized for six weeks,
>how many cops would it take to kill him?

If six New York City cops can sodomize one cabbie with a
>stick, how many cabbies can be brought
>in line for how long?

If six Philadelphia cops can get 6,000 to prop up their frame
>of Mumia Abu-Jamal, how many does it take
>to fix any conviction?

If one professor at Northwestern University can get
>all his journalism students to overturn
>13 death row convictions while the state of Illinois
>pushes through 12 executions, how many years will it
>take till capital punishment is abolished?

If one rich rock and roll songwriter and his band can stir up
>10,000 police, how many poets are needed
>to put an end to injustice?

If it's all just words, like the slogans on police cars,
>investigative reports, trial transcripts, laws
>and the Constitution—just words—
>you got a problem with that?

City of Night

No cool nights in hot cities.
Light always dusty gray, air gritty,
sounds loud and muffled,
people warm and wary.
Love takes place among the ruins,
like trysts at the Coliseum,
sports cars left in the street,
girls in tank tops backed against stone blocks,
guys' jeans hooked behind their knees,
cats watching from damp niches in the walls.

The most important things are said in other languages,
kisses laid on foreign tongues.
The antidote is a walk along the Seine to catch
a homeless artist pretending to work late
against the stone embankment,
listen to young ghosts murmur behind Westminster,
catch the kids on holiday just off the big piazza
imitating colossal statues with dwarfed good humor.

I climb several flights of wooden steps,
sit in a straight chair under a low ceiling
at a cluttered table in a rented space,
blocking out the sound of someone else's TV
and traffic that blows in airless rooms
filled with other people's belongings.
I clear a notebook-sized space,
look out a window facing windows,
and write as though I'm in prison,
just another cage with an open door.

Chusok

I park my car and walk toward the beach.
A soldier looking sixteen climbs down
from a stone wall, steps on his cigaret,
and pushes on his helmet awkwardly.
    "Your car here?" "*Ne.*"
    "Your car not here."
He swept his rifle barrel along barbed wire
down the shoreline, around the point,
and up a rocky hill plunging into the Yellow Sea.

I drive uphill till a break in the pines
above three grassy mounds opens on the Hwang Hae.
Under the hillocks covered by close-clipped grass
lie stories only half the family knows.
These dark vaults are not for foreigner's eyes.
    "Your ancestor not here."

Every autumn at Chusok,
Koreans go home to cultivate graves,
set stones right, open each tomb and inspect the corpses.
    "My uncle is not corrupt," Moon Gi-seok tells me.
    "Two years now and only a little bit of one foot.
    We wrap him again, but no one understands."
Out of a green mound on a Korean hillside
a legend grows about an uncle who will not decay.
Over time this will build tradition,
creating truth out of what no one understands.

I sift my past, broken pieces of a busy life,
all those ashes of burned bridges,
fragments of faces in broken portraits,
and I fancy this is poem fodder.

The guardian demon puts down his torch,
slips on his helmet, raises his sword.
    "You not stop here."
I drive on a way I had not intended
and find something I did not know was here.

Man and Souperman

> *"People like ourselves are best qualified to decide who the people's poet is."*
> —Jack Powers, Kaffe 44, Stockholm, 11/91

Meanwhile, in the background, someone chops vegetables,
the regular whack of a knife on a board in
carrot-length bursts—
quiet, insistent, wholesome.

But we unwrap our words anyway,
pull away plastic and damaged leaves,
lift a pot lid while water heats.

Should we make it new or use the old stock?
Do we have time, before we feed them,
for us to do the cooking?

The tastes of all these people must be satisfied.
The ladle clanks against the sink,
water bubbles, the cook treads softly.

Back in the kitchen someone makes soup,
not from stones or imaginary potatoes.
We have real potatoes all around us.

They are only potatoes, yes,
but with a little skill,
the people can have real soup.

Human Engineering

> *In human engineering, the potter's wheel showed little promise of the clocks and turbines that were to derive from it; no more do the comparatively simple structures of early burrowers hint at the complex organs and complex animals, including ourselves, made possible by a hollow body."*—Nigel Calder, *The Life Game: Evolution and the New Biology*

Drag bags of clay in from the shed
and set your foot to time on the treadle,
turn discordant mud to musical shape,
draw awkward pieces through the hollow pipes
set in the earthen ends of organs we
have become: orifices for silence.

Turbines were promised by the potter's wheel
because clockwork regulates those echoes
in the vacant tube: in dissonant soup
surrounded by primal muck we could
only burrow for solace and inform
the hungry night with ordered quiet.

Not entropy, static set to pictures,
but symphonies of calm we must become,
concerted spheres whose melody when seen
has greater depth than those who hear can feel:
the modeled earth of a Korean vase filled
with the hand music of the potter's art,

fired notes greater than indelicate
tongues can sound. A man plucks the ecliptic
and the galaxy stands in tune. Join me:
I'll bow Saturn, you beat the moon, a gong,
and the organized universe will sit
and watch the silence of our needful song.

A Pleasant Young Man

We take a pleasant young man
from the middle of the country. His
greatest skill—how to get along
with the majority—was learned in junior high.
His greatest talent—taking a good picture.
He sits behind a massive desk,
the smooth button at his elbow
not even sullied by lint from his
expensive suit, and we know that
as sure as a kid with a gun will have
to pull the trigger, he will manipulate
an excuse to push it.

We keep the buttons
away from generals, we have not yet
learned to govern without the gadgets
that make governing fun for little boys.
With the unerring accuracy of the ninth-grade
class president, he singles out the guy
everybody can hate, the foreign language poet,
the sad kid who cannot do anything
about accidents of birth, and when the time
is right, when the danger is minimal,
the crowd has leaned, the votes are needed,
Presto!

Missile batteries become junk.
Did anyone stand guard?
The munitions stockpile explodes.
How many worked there?
The rebel camps are leveled.
Was there anyone at home?
Any women cooking dinner,
children playing in the yards?
The young man's majority holds
its breath for a moment, relaxes
when the world does not explode,

and cannot make the connection
years later when maimed children
with foreign tongues blow up
barracks full of boys and girls,
airliners fall out of skies,
or an affable young man drops
on top of pieces of his head
in the back of a limousine.

Galileo's Apology

A message in a bottle

You denied the facts; so I insisted on facts.
Flyspecks in this tepid soup, you couldn't
understand the earth will make a slight hiss
dropped into the fiery cauldron of the sun,
and never imagined the truth of metaphor.

Love is the morning and the evening star.
Hot suns nourish as well as burn.
The moon's silver disk, the flat face of consistency.
The war planet dried and dead beyond Egypt's desert.
Great stormy Jupiter neither star nor earth,
the essential orbiter unable to choose.

And others undreamed of in your time:
periods of comets defying your calendars,
galactic shapes more varied than the creatures of the sea,
dust cloud expanses larger than we have concepts for,
vague angel asteroids time travelers bump into.
Beyond those, the mysteries...

Leprous stars pulse madly, black spots engulf all
whiteness in one fist. Set your theories, raise your swords,
scepters, threats and power. Out my prison window
I see symphonic harmony unfinished because
its instruments have not yet been invented.

Dispute how celestial bodies move. A child's puzzle.
Beyond childhood's end and your puny adolescence,
the meaning is a golden book of signs made sense
by yielding its truth, accepting its way, understanding
anyone's place, and loving whatever put us here,
amphibians in a lukewarm soup, struggling to comprehend
the parting of the waters, the separation of light from darkness,
the attraction and orbit of things and what they mean.

Frederick Douglass

*"Humanity, justice and liberty demand
the service of the living voice."*

I have no ancestry but memory.
What befalls my children is my history.
Find my forebears in rocks, trees and the voice
of the wind. I sprang full grown by my choice
from my throat. Raised by strangers, early I
learned that my chart would be my words. My cry
cut chains, raised a northern beacon we
still follow in these days, fatherless but free.

I took what Nature gave me, breathing
righteous angry life into it and wreathing
the indifferent heads of the white world round
with prickly principle to bow them down.
My speaking created time; my writing defeated days.
The right time to oppose injustice is always.

Delta Evening

I fill the noisy void of evening
by licking my funky fingertips.
Smashing my head through
plasterboard walls.

I need suspenders for my bowels
every time I get hit by a truck
with a great seal on its side door.

Arguments among the chamber of deputies
ranged across the back of my skull
interrupt jumbled reading:
I submit to note taking
for my unconscious.

I find no comfort among the bones
with which they have lined my room.

When I finally run mad into the swamp,
scattering cottonmouth and alligator
with my manic screaming, stopping
to drink feverishly at infested pools,
the fools have already moved
upstream to pollute the water.

The Martin Bormann Dog Care Book

1. Kinder, Kirche, Küche

When Leni brought the dog
and the dog book home a year ago,
K. was sitting dully in the old stuffed chair
watching the cloth-covered speaker
say in its national voice:
Each victory brings greater opportunity
for us to do the people's will,
and K. thought how the present points always
to what has been and what might have been.

Leni put the puppy, an old bed toy,
and a clock wrapped in a blanket scrap
in a cardboard box in the kitchen
and sat down to read: For proper training
construct situations to produce unwanted behavior
which you punish.

     K. leaned back,
an eye on part of the 20th century
squeezed between commercials—
penniless old men in gassy residue
frigid from transportation on the 6 o'clock news.
The speaker said: *We need not rely on*
police power when the mandate to govern
comes from the people.

     When the news ended,
Leni asked K. to buy a choke chain because
the book said: Behavior is controlled by pain.

K. looked out the window,
seeing first her reflection in the kitchen light
holding the book demurely,
like a nun without her underwear,
then through her, adolescent wraiths
hungry in their sexuality

roaming the night with bobbing heads
and said, "We should
settle one thing about the dog for good."

By a bonfire on the corner
young men in work shirts
danced to the beat on institutional drums
while from the living room the voice said:
Our system of competition insures the drive
for the strong to survive.

"She won't get too big,
and I'll have company
and feel safer while you're away."

K. looked at the large brown paws,
shook his head and knew
a chain wouldn't do.

"It has to be a chain. The book says:
The chain must tighten on command
and go slack when you relax your hand."

K. nodded, his ear to the station:
This campaign has been conducted
so as not to divide the nation

    2. *Ordnung muss sein.*

Leni fidgeted in the flickering light
waiting for K. When she heard him coming,
she walked heavily to the lighted doorway
to meet him outside and talk to him there.

"The dog is gone."
                        She saw the lunch pail
in his hand and sat on the steps
while he stood there
looking into the backyard evening.

"The book said not to chase her,
  but to punish her when she came to me."
He shifted tiredly, wondering if
the burning twilight would flash
on every window in the row, and said,
to keep the growing silence from saying
there was nothing to be said,
"Fixing her is best, you know.
She'll still be a good pet.
Doesn't the book say so?"

                                     "Yes,
but then she won't be good for show."

"Still, we might try—for us—
the rest is not our business."

When all the windows had burned out,
the voice hung palpably in the air:
It is our job to keep the country
from rule by the mob.

       3. *Arbeit macht frei.*

To make ends meet, Leni gets a job.
Getting up long before work
to bathe, powder, and deodorize,
she sets her hair in intricate ringlets,
leaving notes for K. to walk the dog.

He comes home for dinner
and dozes through the news:
This is a great victory
because it will benefit all of us,
the common people.

                    K. reads on his own:

Genetic breeding facilitates
the owner's job in selecting mates.

6 nights a week the butcher paints her body
gold as the rims on dinner plates
and helps her mount the platform
where she poses and rotates.

The safest rule in breeding laws
is to keep your bitch away from other dogs.

Only twice in 6 months has the bouncer
had to stop a patron who tried to mount her.
Leni likes the afternoons for shopping,
and K. likes reading: For show or sale
the rule is the same: never castrate a male.

Each night she is in heat
K. parades her through the neighborhood
assessing the males for likely mates;
if she moves out of line, he stops
and jerks the chain.

                              If she won't breed,
a professional can implant the seed.

Leni is arrested
and on the lino-topped table
in the police station basement
they rape her.

The next time the bitch is in heat,
K. comes home and finds her body in the street.

4. Ein Volk, Ein Reich, Ein Führer

*After such a long campaign
it is hard to argue with results.*

Reflected in the glass that night,
tongue out, only a trace of blood,
K. sees her wrapped in a sheet

and thinks, another dog, perhaps.

He is late for work on cloudy days.

Well-trained, he should stay at his station
no matter what the temptation.
K. writes his name at night
and reads it back in morning,
winds her pillow in her yellow robe
and puts his head beneath it
when he sleeps.

*We must unite
behind the strongest, the most fearless,
the most temperate leader of our time.*

He wants to stay at home,
afraid of the young men
who walk the town in groups of ten,
and so he draws the curtains
and the outdoors disappears.

A command must be obeyed, or persist
until he chokes into unconsciousness.

He cannot set the clock aright
for fear that it might cut his hands.

Perfectly timed, without apparent call,
security men come in and line the hall.

He needs blackness, a printer's invention,
as a passport for his own intention.

As the people come to know him better,
they will come to love him more.

He takes off his watch
and his hand falls to the floor;

he puts his foot on it
to stop it crawling out the door.

Behavior must be predictable
or he should be destroyed.

He reached to change the station
but the set wasn't on.

We can only wait and see
what this landslide victory
will do to his personality.

Over and Over

An aging poet and teacher born in 1940,
who fought against Vietnam at home
and for civil rights in the cities,
have I increased my chances next life
of coming back as a holy man, a woman, a gazelle?

That is progress on this wheel—
most of us stuck in millennial rounds
as fast food clerks notching paper crowns for spoiled kids,
spinning mill spindle girls, charcoal makers,
mud-carrying coolies, mastodon bait.

Born in 1840 I took a day and a half to die at Shiloh,
      parched, blind, baked in dry rough wool, basted in my
      blood.
In 1740, fevered on a foul ship in foreign waters,
      driven by a cutting lash to climb high spars,
      I lost my grip in a yaw and fell to the wooden deck,
      smashing my skull like an egg.
In Bavaria in 1640 it took me two weeks to die from blood
      poisoning when an oxcart crushed my leg
      and animal shit entered my blood.
In 1540 a Cossack stomped me because he was drunk and I
      was not.
In 1440 large black blood-filled globules burst the skin
      of my underarms and groin.
In 1340 an Asian horseman took my head for scimitar practice.
In 1240 Christians trampled me in the road.
In 1140 a fever within a week of birth. 1040 at birth.
940 at birth.
840 at birth.
740 I can't remember. 640 I can't remember.
But, of course, you can't remember that I lived.

I was a pitch blender in the Phoenician trade,
      a blood stain under a pyramid block,
      scattered bones in a Yangtze dam,

      torn by sharks after a typhoon,
      somebody's idea of dog food.

Once in a distant historical instant, I was lifted
on murmured prayers and adored, the precious future
of a group of cousins who valued their families as much as
      sunlight,
but that was only in a small out-of-the-way place
      before what you call *civilization*.

Face It

The CAT scan operator
fits the leg block so the gown will creep.
The ultrasound tech oils my body,
rubs the vibrator, watches the picture, and
glances up to read my face between the lines.
Rafael, the best MRI man in town,
won't look anywhere but in my eyes
when he talks to me.

The mysteries of the heart
may be plumbed with certainty
by anyone with a magnetic field.
Sources of bile and phlegm, blood and urine,
can be mapped to their inmost secretions,
But who can trust what the face says
when it has been programmed all its life
to be read on screens as it wants to be seen?

Time was we could see
the madness in the lunatic's glance,
doubt in the lover's look.
But if the liar tells us truthfully,
the judge sober with his thumb on the scales,
the politician repeat that he is not a crook,
the unchallenged broadcast becomes the truth.

We have learned *not* to tell how a thief looks
when our wallet is gone, the banks empty,
corporate execs drunk on tropical shores,
the country at war, and the government
has revised how not-a-crook looks.

War

When asked if I'd fight for my country, I told the FBI, "Yea. I will point a gun for my country, But I won't guarantee you which way."
—Woody Guthrie

King Philip's Head

A sign of victory, power, and warning,
The head sat on a pike in Plymouth Village
Until it became a familiar thing—
One generation scarred, another
Scared, and the third laughed at it.
After that, scalps were collected from everyone.

Women and children were mostly that "everyone,"
But who knows death smells a warning
For hell-fearing settlers to beware of it.
After birds pecked the face clean, the village
Kids still held their noses, and elders knew another
Was not needed for the point made by this one.

Those serious natives comprehended a complete thing,
Or laughed at what amused everyone
Or stared deep into forest and sea, another
Silent way in which settlers beheld a warning
That power could overwhelm their village
And with natural finality, end it.

The rotted face exorcised their terror.
It Stood until the totem was just a thing,
A powerless token that a village
Hunted down and killed what everyone
Had feared. It was a victory, a power, but no warning
To all that there would never be another.

Did it stand over there in a separate Place?
What time saw the remove of it?
Why was there no more need for warning?
No one knows for sure what happened to the thing.
We have only written words for everyone
Who comes to hear about Plymouth Village.

In the history passed down from town
To city, we hold this fact to stop another

Revisionist idea—that natives were equal to everyone.
Philip was no king, and children must take it
Seriously that he was finally just a thing,

And with all who followed, sufficient warning.
Of another noble concept we have made a lesser
And destroyed the power and beauty in it for everyone.
A warning, how a noble experiment became an ignorant village.

In Memory

The weather never changes
although places dry up and shrink.
Big public events stand,
the burning towers of Sodom and Gomorrah
above everyday lives that vanish.
That is what Lot's family knows
because they went on
and looked back in later days.

History does not tell us
where those collapsed cities lie.
What calamities marked many lives
mean nothing unearthed
or when some strayed diver
finds the infrastructure of dead coral
to be not bed rock but skyline.

No one knows what city Lot's wife
stood on when she looked back.
We know the frozen one
who lives in tales we tell each generation,
making of her misdeed
the lonely warning of a roadside hazard
where no roads now run.

How evil were they for modern times?
What righteous destruction
was called down by their ways?
Or were they less evil in a time
when God had some hope
we would take heed?
So unlike today,
when holy people wield God's sword
and the wicked rain destruction on their lands.

The Whiskey Rebellion

You want a big tree
with branches wide and high,
a huge trunk so no one will see

even when they're nigh,
near a supply of hickory, ash and oak,
hardwoods seasoned and dry

or they'll catch you by the smoke.
What else is a man to do?
This whiskey tax is no joke,

and he needs things to see him through—
anesthetics for the pain,
an antidote for the flu,

a wee bit for the brain.
We didn't get rid of those Tories
to tax ourselves again.

I don't believe those stories
that government knows for the best.
If they had so much for their glories,

they can give a poor man some rest.
We've got to set the bit for the horse.
We can't all move out west.

And these things never go their course
till we make them know what we see.
If we must use force,

let us decide how it will be,
or we'll soon be impressed in their wars;
we'll soon be shipped out to sea,

caught on the edges of foreign shores
for some other fluid's other reasons,
to settle another tyrant's scores.

Gettysburg

> *July 1*

Not all first days of battle are tenuous,
but this one was. Probing skirmishers,
casualties, stern calls for support units,
frantic searches for ammunition and supplies
punctuated by the whistle and thud of artillery
and the clank and jingle of rigging, shouts
in the short nervous night before the day
when you know someone must try something.

Newly-breveted Col. Charles Whitten found time
in fading daylight to write Sophia on Nantucket.
Orlando Brewster judged the distance to a small
ravine, a short stretch of creek, patch of woods,
and a run to freedom in the confusion. General Lee
did not like the terrain, but nobody ever let him choose
where to fight the inevitable battles. Four or five
days from now his troops will have won this war
or lost this fight. In the town, a war widow looks
out a second story window, fretting about
rebel troops marching through Gettysburg.

> *July 2*

The armies, not yet at full force,
carry forward on momentum
or seize the high ground and prepare. It has
been decided who will be aggressor, defender,
which topography will determine glory, carnage,
and they edge right and left, seeking which loose
ends can be turned to advantage.

Col. Whitten's note gets posted. Brewster refines
his timing. Lee sees how it must be fought.
A council of union generals agrees on what

they must hold. Because she cannot sleep
for the sound of supply trains and wagons,
the widow studies the glow of campfires in summer heat,
smoke and dust irritating her breathing until
she falls asleep, her head on the window sill.

July 3

This is the day no one could have predicted.
Two vast complex organisms face each other
on open ground, one determined to win,
the other not to lose. With little advantage
on either side, the Gods of War roll the dice.

Col. Whitten's writing hand is shot off in mid-air.
Longstreet's delay brings Brewster's horse up front
and condemns him to two more years of hungry slavery.
Lee's mistake! By evening, the widow has learned
to measure the conflict by wounded men in her street
and a great moaning quiet where last night's campfires burned.

Dry Tank

When rookies invaded his space at the bar,
veterans said leave him alone. He spoke
in a register nobody used. After the raid
when no one else returned, our crew never
worried about war again. In flak he flew
to daylight. He knew what fighters did.
They called him Dry Tank because
in the Battle of Britain, he was last down.
He wore out every plane he flew. We stayed
as long as we could; it was safer than rotating
into another. We knew all the names
of the war machine we had to defeat,
and could do it with him in the seat.
I saw him once when he flew jets, but they
kept him out of Korea. It wasn't a war.

All Quiet

I can't care how fine the film
rude or realistic cinema is clean
gruesome in gas masks skulls show terror
not what I know but really the rats
millions of murdered wrapped up in wire
tiered under tents a fair feast indeed
but nobody knows how to show smells
rotten sweet stomachs cordite in clusters
but, God, the gas that winded our way
any little bit like it my head is up high
where's the way out gagging not gone
you think you'd survive having handled exhaust
cigarette smoke industrial air
one puny puff that was what hit me
one big one should have strangled me sure
fill a room full of aught but air
I sit and I see it caged in my chair
in an oxygen tent a skull with a stare

Turtles

A column of pedestrians twelve wide
and six deep floods the street
when crossing signals sound.
Lines at taxi stands are 25 fares long.
People stream beneath colorful canopies
past dry goods and plastic ware,
handcarts full of silver mackerel,
dried pewter fish, shrimp-tinted squid,
gnarled octopus, sprouts, grains,
beans, seaweed, piles of chickens,
and families of goats.

Inside the newspaper,
behind the shell of the TV screen,
I hardly heard the siren,
but Chung, who had just remarked
how Nammun is always crowded
heard, and the city changed, as if
the turtles that ward off destruction
had lifted their heads.

One wail and three-fourths of the people
are gone. Most of the rest are going
with small, quick deliberate steps,
except an old man scraping stone,
his beard an inverted *fleur-de-lis*,
a businessman looking bored and Japanese,
a few soldiers at ease as only 16-year olds can be.

Loudspeakers bark vaguely. Chung says,
"Maybe a North Korean plane.
Inchon and Suwon are on alert.
This is not a drill." Titanium pencils
fly over and break the cool blue
air into clamoring pieces.

When I was a pointy-headed child,
I fought for light during blackouts
and my old man was a boring warden.
These people have no time for that.
If some MIG jockey
dumps a thousand pounder in the next block,
rescuers must face north first.

Under the sheet metal carapace of the bus,
kids twist quietly. The woman in blue
satin bites the side of her thumb.
We stretch our necks to hear the radio
with more than six o'clock curiosity.
High in the afternoon flies a B-52,
the final turtle of man-made destruction.

Kwag calls and through the rattling shell
tells me a Chinese plane has landed
at the US base—at least that's what
he heard, he says, with the skepticism
of a man who has ears for the news
and eyes on the turtles.

Dave's Cave

Old Soldier's Night, South Boston, December, 1996

For some kids it's not a party till they go to the basement.
Barely survivors of childhood's end,
we ask permission so wary wives and friends will know.
A guy with shoulder-length hair says,
"You need a haircut."
"I was on my way," I say, "before Dave waylaid me."

In a knee-tight rectangle of chairs at
a case set upside down, its top holding
a double-lipped glass ash tray.
Ehrhart grumbles amid the clutter, "Everything except match-
    es."
A box of wooden ones stands atop
a steel file and within minutes two joints circulate
in opposite directions among half a dozen guys.

Fold this scene over on itself in fractured cubist time.
Dim lights show a high basement with the household goods
of three families stacked to head height, hedging
a tight square of men and women desperate for inside safety,
brain relief from good lives rising in monthly increments
to wall off fears from a previous crease.

Fold that into a tight dark bunker,
dirt and sweat, shelves to cover their heads
on days when incoming shredded buddies,
tore air through flesh, left rosary beads of blood,
cloth, tiny brown joints passed from fingertip to fingertip.

No one ever said, "This is hell," but
everyone referred back to "the World,"
the seam between the two
like a line in a kid's game nobody
could cross without some arbitrary permission.
"Mother, may I?" when mother was your CO,

an AK-47, a terrified voice at the end of a tin telephone.
"What are you afraid of, voice? I'm the one who's out here."

The line was a trip wire, a curtain of napalm,
paddy dike or jungle fringe,
a piece of paper torn from a book no one could read,
hidden in the mind of one of those little people in black
      pajamas.
Fold along that line and the top comes down,
rickety brick pillars supporting cross beams, planks and sand
      bags.

In this ritual circle we murmur laconic incantations,
pass the shit, love the comfort of a dark cave
among a few of our own kind
in a place terrible beyond our imaginings,
where other kids with childishly accented voices call,
"Come out, come out,
wherever you are."

The Last Nightmare

*for Al Schultz, a former student
killed in Vietnam, August, 1967*

He sleeps peacefully in
the last nightmare of the night,
the one remembered when startled awake,
charged with the fright
of one killed violently,
the ghost wandering the world in fear.

He sleeps in
a woodcut printed on a canvas wall;
pure light flashes and shakes
a high-pitched wail
fluttering to his clean head;
the black and gray crosshatch
splinters white,
increasing to a scream,
slashing blood to steam.

He sleeps—
woodcut ripped,
curtain broken—
head alone on a pillow stripped;
dogtags on a torn neck.

What Old Men Know

Firewalls, paper shredders, and microwaves,
in general what's wrong with cars and trucks
but not enough to fix the new ones.
Experts at commercial driving, booze, geology,
land and law, but never enough about women.
Besides knowing what their numbers mean,
they calculate fruit and oatmeal,
which dogs to have and which ones to avoid,
when to challenge a waitress or offer concern,
how to stay warm at night, where to fish,
and how to find out without prying.

They know what it means when a wife
comes home from the hospital and isn't going back.
Every one of them has suffered indignities
of proctology, colonoscopy, and a physicians' questioning look.
They wear their wrinkles and scars as easily as flannel shirts.
They measure their time in meals and miles,
their stature in town by who is glad to see them coming.
They won't see much of their children
until they have to move in with them.
They know the young are most affected by war,
learning lessons no one wants, and they can't change it.

Absalom, Absalom

Northwest wind rattles the shutters;
snow cushions street sounds
while trees creak and clatter against a window caked with ice.
Associating this scene with Faulkner's novel,
I think of my son living most of his life
in cheap apartments atop three flights of wooden stairs—
isolate, creative, longing for a few things
the world will never give him.
Some of us are born for sacrifice,
and even if our fathers would be kings,
they cannot stop it.
         Oh, Absalom, my son.
That would have been your name
if I had had my way. Or Abraham.
Which the greater pain, to be the son
who his father cannot save
or the father slitting the son's throat?

I made tentative steps toward the soldier's way
to visit my anger in vengeful Armageddon on the world,
then pulled back before the awful realities of masquerades.
I never woke on Ash Wednesday with limbs and torsos
of honest folk piled in bloody array around me,
my motley costume singed, mud-caked,
felt my wide eyes invaded by death,
staring as some half-brained mummer
pinned a gaudy star on my hollow chest
and urged me to rise and rejoin the slaughter.

Once again I feel a bond halfway around the earth
while I hunch over a desk in a warm garret
under a snow-covered roof. He sprawls
in desert sand smelling diesel and rocket fuel,
ordnance rattling in cacophonous air,
squinting across no-man's land,
tasting blood lust risen in his throat,
the hatred he would die to unleash on his brother

whose father also sits at a desk—
an Arabic scribbler proud he never killed,
ashamed he cannot save any of those dearest ones
because they have elevated their love and hate
of him to God's will.
    Oh, Absalom, my son.

At the Table

> *Tomorrow,*
> *I'll sit at the table When company comes. Nobody'll dare*
> *Say to me,*
> *'Eat in the kitchen,'*
> *Then.*
> —from "Epilogue" by Langston Hughes

Once you get the explosives,
the rest is simple—batteries,
speaker wire, a mercury switch
from a thermostat or stereo.
Strap it to yourself under loose clothes
and stroll in the market.

It's no more complex than British officers
tying Hindu rebels across cannons and firing a salvo,
the SS machine gunning civilians on the edges of a mass graves,
Japanese soldiers executing citizens
with shots to the backs of their heads,
Serb commanders ordering mass rape of Muslim villages,
Israeli tanks shooting three girls and a school teacher,
our own Sand Creek, My Lai, Waco, or desert wars.

Unconnected in foreign cities, I go to market.
In Korea, bananas cost a dollar, apples a quarter.
In Taipeh, it's opposite,
but everywhere there are
apples and bananas,
citrus and squash,
fish and chickens.
No matter what strange lands,
I stand on my home planet.

I found no perversity when my host
in Jerusalem told me the market
I walked through was the one
they often blew up.

Those who can afford it rebuild;
those without must make them pay.

A 17-year-old Palestinian sits
on a straight chair at a Formica-topped table,
precious Semtex next to a mercury tube,
short wires in hand,
lovely eyes glowing with focused hatred.

His grandfather was the leading automobile
importer in the Middle East before 1950.
While the remnants of his family huddled
in a shattered apartment in Beirut,
his father delivered pizzas in Arkansas
and went to night school with a Biafran,
a German communist, a Chinese poet,
an African-American school teacher from Texas,
and none of them had to explain anything to the others.

Those in the kitchen must find a way
to get the attention of those who talk
so militantly about the good *they* do,
the necessity of *their* killing,
the glory of *their* labor.
If not, pray your son will have another
before a handsome young man
pulls the chair to his table
and twists the wire to the switch.

Priests' Skulls

"Hell is paved with priests's skulls," *
cut to fit by demon masons,
laid gently in place by nuns' hands,
and soldiers' boots have worn them flat.

The archbishop of Madrid blessed fascist cannons.
The cardinal of Berlin admired newly acquired art
and chatted with Hitler about ethnic purity laws.
What the Pope can't see can't be pointed to.

First the Jews and gypsies go.
When the war goes badly, Nazis disappear,
and no one can say where anyone went.
Trains run to Auschwitz and to Switzerland.

Mass deaths draw crowds out of Serb towns;
rosaries dangle from bloody hands.
Scapulars and blessed medals

Ministers foam at the mouth with oaths
against strongest enemies, weakest friends.
Add another bead to the charm bracelet:
Carthage, Jerusalem, Carcassonne, Mostar.

A Rwandan nun sprays huts with holy water,
screams at the devil in arms wielding Hutu machetes,
justifies God's destruction in hands firing Tutsi guns,
with never enough salt to sow bloody ground.

Priests in eternal fire give each other absolution.
Burning nuns lay hot bones in mocking patterns—
swastikas, stars of David, fasces, crosses—
crushed into paving by military boots.
"Christ! What are patterns for?" **

                          *John Chrysostum
                          **Amy Lowell

Like Kings

Like old kings in Shakespeare, muttering a bit
second thoughts about regicide,
his half wit council urges on our royal nit wit.

Let its cry for change abate while it
musters failed policy and shattered pride
like old kings in Shakespeare, muttering a bit.

Still, it's we who will not see how unfit
we are to criticize, as from inside,
his half wit council urges on our royal nit wit.

We get the news, watch sports, and sit
in quiet while madmen push war for our side
like old kings in Shakespeare, muttering a bit.

Too many do little or go along with it,
the war plans, stupidity too gross to hide,
his half wit council urges on our royal nit wit.

We love our play stations, cars, flags, and shit,
so we smile and let them decide.
Like old kings in Shakespeare, muttering a bit
his half wit council urges on our royal nit wit.

ACKNOWLEDGEMENTS

"Room," *Extension* (San Francisco: Idlewild, 1969) and *Anon* (Ann Arbor: spring, 1969).

"The Brown Bug," *Since Feeling Is First* (Scott, Foresman, 1972).

"Collaboration," *Poetry &* (Chicago, November, 1976), I, 5. "The Martin Bormann Dog Care Book," *Oyez Review* (Chicago, 1979).

"The Potter's Mistress," *Another Chicago Magazine* IV (1979) and in *The Inspired Pen* to accompany *The Inspired Hand V*, University of Southern Maine, Lewiston-Auburn College, January-March, 2012).

"Deterrence" and "Turtles," *Menagerie*, fall, 1987. "The Comedian," *Amandla Ngwethu!* I, 1 (spring, 1991).

"Absalom, Absalom" and "The Aluminum Helmet," *Falling Wallendas* (Chicago: Tia Chucha, 1994).

"28 Things for White People to Do during Black History Month," WMFO-FM (January 24, 1994) and *MAP of Austin Poetry*, #297-1 (February 9, 2004).

"Killers," *Kameleon* (Beverly, MA, fall, 1990) XIII; *Pressed Streets* (winter1996-97), I, 1; and *Mantis* (Stanford, 2000), 72).

"A Pleasant Young Man," *Point Blank* (1997).

"A Mournful Wail," *Sensations* 17 (winter, 1997). "Over and Over," *The Umbrella*, I, 8 (August, 1999) and *The South Boston Literary Gazette*, IV (winter 2001).

"City of Night," *The MAP of Austin Poetry*, 99 (September 27, 1999).

"Frayed Plaid Robes," *Children Remember Their Fathers* (Seattle: Gazoobi Tales, 2000).

"Miss Brooks," *Another Chicago Magazine* III (1978); Illinois Arts Council Literary Award 1979; *Best of MAP of Austin Poetry*, IV, 2000-2001.

"Native Art," *Pembroke Magazine* 4 (1973), 112; and *The Confidence Man* (Princeton: Ragged Sky, 2006).

"Galileo's Apology," *Sensations* 23 (fall, 2001). "Priests's Skulls," *100 Poets Against the War* (Cambridge, England: Salt, 2003).

"King Philip's Head," "The Whiskey Rebellion," and "Frederick Douglass," *Sensations Magazine* 30 (summer, 2003).

"All Quiet," "Dry Tank," "Dave's Cave," "Absalom," "East St. Louis, 1917," and "Like Kings" *Sensa- tions Magazine* 31 (fall, 2003).

"Tender Analysis," *Mosaic* (spring, 2004), 16.

"The Badger and the Bear," "The Emotions of

Dreams," "The Fiery Furnace," and "Star Dance," *Sensations Magazine* 40 (2006).

"Any Summer Day," *Mulberry Poets and Writers Journal*, VII, 1 (fall, 2006).

"Parents Held Hostage by Hatless Teen," *Eating Her Wedding Dress* (Princeton: Ragged Sky, 2009).

BIOGRAPHY

When Michael Brown graduated from college in 1962 he moved immediately to Philadelphia and enrolled in the Intern Teaching Program at Temple University. In September he started teaching at Central High. After one semester he was offered one of several places. He chose William Penn High, an all-black high school for girls north of center city. The school had a good reputation among teachers, but what could he do for those women? It became apparent that no one was teaching writing. Doing that would make the students employable. When they began writ- ing, he began, too.

By 1965 he moved to Pennsbury High in Bucks County. After two years there, with his master's degree and a couple of summers teaching at Temple, he sought a doctoral program to certify his right to teach teachers. The University of Michigan enrolled him in a double major in English and Education. The times also engaged him in campus politics, and his writing took a political turn. He proudly turned in a dissertation on the poets of the Harlem Renaissance, directed by Robert Hayden.

By 1970 he was hired by East Texas State University to head a Ph.D. program in the teaching of English. He also published his first poems. In a succession of jobs through the 1970s he moved to Central (Ohio) State, Western Michigan University, and the University of Illinois at Chicago. By 1980 he was teaching in a storefront managed by a community organization. He was also writing for the Chicago Reader and the Chicago Tribune.

In the 1980s Chicago State, a university mostly for African American women, hired him to teach varieties of literature and writing, then an exchange professor in South Korea for two years, and finally Chair of the Composition program.

By 1990 he became involved with the poetry slam, married the best-known performer, and moved with her to Boston. He taught in a variety of higher education institutions, settling finally at Mount Ida College, where he established himself as Director of the Communications Program. Meanwhile, he and his wife started the Boston Poetry Slam at the Cantab, a venue that continues today. Such prominence in slam and poetry brought trips to Europe, including exchanges with Irish artists and coordinating the first Poetry Olympics in Stockholm. His *Falling Wallendas* (1994) was published by Tia Chucha and is in its second printing of a thousand. That was followed by *Susquehanna* (Ragged Sky) and *The Man Who Makes Amusement Rides* (Hanover) both in 2003. *The Confidence Man* (Ragged Sky) came out in 2006.

In 2007, he and his wife Valerie Lawson moved to downeast Maine, where they own 40 mostly wooded acres with a smattering of blueberries and retired sled dogs. For eight years they published the poetry quarterly *Off the Coast*, and now run Resolute Bear Press. Their front windows look across Passamaquoddy Bay to St. Andrews, New Brunswick. Michael continues to teach and write. *The Martin Bormann Dog Care Book* is a collection of political poems written over the last 50 years.

www.ingramcontent.com/pod-product-compliance
Lightning Source LLC
Chambersburg PA
CBHW030441010526
44118CB00011B/737